HOW TO SCRAPE SKIES

Jefferson

Washington

Franklyn

Portrait of the authors

HOW TO
SCRAPE SKIES

The United States explored,
rediscovered and explained

GEORGE MIKES

Nicolas Bentley
drew the pictures

London
ALLAN WINGATE

First published in Mcmxlviii
by Allan Wingate (Publishers) Ltd
12 Beauchamp Place London SW3

Second Impression October 1948
Third Impression August 1949
Fourth Impression February 1950
Fifth Impression August 1950
Sixth Impression January 1952
Seventh Impression November 1952
Eighth Impression November 1953
Ninth Impression November 1954
Tenth Impression February 1956

Composed in Monotype
Perpetua and Cartoon types

Printed in Great Britain by
Spottiswoode Ballantyne & Co Ltd
London and Colchester

'My country, 'tis of thee
Sweet land of liberty,
Of thee I sing;
Land where my fathers died,
Land of the pilgrims' pride,
From every mountain side
Let freedom ring.'

Samuel Francis Smith: America

By the same author :

HOW TO BE AN ALIEN
WISDOM FOR OTHERS
MILK AND HONEY
DOWN WITH EVERYBODY !
SHAKESPEARE AND MYSELF
ÜBER ALLES
EIGHT HUMORISTS
LITTLE CABBAGES

CONTENTS

PREFACE

AFTER the appearance of my little educational treatise *How to be an Alien,* I was bitterly reproached by a number of people for having written the book at all. 'Who wants to be an alien?' people asked me indignantly. 'We all want to be Americans. All of us: the two thousand million non-American population of this earth, children of all ages, continents, sexes and religious denominations; rich and poor, old and young, black and white, small and great. The coming century is going to be the century of the Americans.' 'You are wrong'—I objected—'it is going to be the century of the common man.' 'Same thing,' they retorted. 'Aren't the Americans common enough?'

Well, I have always wanted to be a man with a mission; the only difficulty was deciding what my mission should be. There it was now, my great opportunity—to tell people how to be Americans.

I should like to assure readers before going any further that they may rely on my guidance. I spent two full months in the United States, studying their history, economics, politics, ethnography, constitution, race-problems, legislative, executive and juridical institutions, as well as American social life, geology, genealogy and anthropology. I talked (personally) to many people; travelled across the Manhattan peninsula a dozen times; went for a great number of car and subway rides, visited the Bronx and Queens and reached the outskirts of Brooklyn. What is more, my vision and judgement were not obscured by any previous knowledge of the United States, personal or otherwise.

I travelled widely in New York State; I saw New Jersey, Pennsylvania, Maryland, Washington D.C., Virginia, Connecticut and Massachusetts. I stood at the border and looked right into the depths of West Virginia, and I dare say it looked quite a problem. I talked to people (personally or on the telephone) who had come from as far away as California, Oregon and Washington—without D.C.—and I spent three full days studying the subcontinent of Canada.

Nevertheless, in spite of such thoroughgoing preparation for and devotion to my task, I found myself confronted with certain serious difficulties. First of all, it is not easy to spot America. In New York you will be told that New York is not America. Should you then ask any question concerning the Negro problem in the South, it will be instantly explained to you that the South is not America; New England is so terribly British (because they say tomahto instead of tomayto and sometimes potahto instead of potayto) that it cannot possibly be regarded as America; the Wild West is too wild, the Mid-West is too Mid-Western, and Hollywood—well Hollywood, of course, has never been America. In general, big cities such as Chicago (pronounced Shicago) Philadelphia, Boston, Detroit, Los Angeles, San Francisco etc are not America because America is essentially a rural country; on the other hand, the United States without these vast cities is just not America.

You will find it equally difficult to identify an American. People, all of whose great grand parents were born in the United States, will explain to you that they are Irish, Dutch or Swedes. (Everybody is something else.) The only people who call themselves Americans straightforwardly are those who became citizens five or ten minutes ago.

However, only the superficial observer will be misled into believing that there is no such thing as the United States and the American people. They do indeed exist. They have produced the American constitution, the

American way of life, the comic strips in their newspapers; they have their national game, baseball—which is cricket played with a strong American accent—and they have a national language, entirely their own, unlike any other language spoken on this earth.

On board R.M.S. *Queen Elizabeth*, May 1947

G. M.

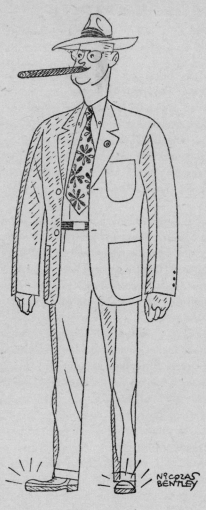

Swell guy

I. APÉRITIF

A SWELL GUY

IN America, shoes shine almost as brilliantly as trousers do in post-war England. Only the most careful and determined person can avoid having his shoes cleaned four or five times a day at stands, in shoe-repair shops, at the barber's and in the street. The Americans are a shoe-conscious nation. Only a small band of distinguished, rich and conservative New Englanders try to maintain the noble tradition of dirty shoes, Sunday and weekday rags and an unshaven chin.

In England, I used to be a moderately, or at least tolerably, well-dressed man. Upon my arrival in America, however, my brother besought me urgently to go and buy new clothes; I looked, he said, like a beggar of very mediocre abilities and of the lower beggar income brackets. (In America, everybody belongs to a certain income bracket.)

Here is the rule:

Discard all your shirts and buy new ones—red shirts with huge black checks or, if desired, circles; purple shirts with olive-green butterflies painted all over them, or sky-blue shirts with brown fish. Get some neckties, too—for instance one divided horizontally into blue and golden sections, full of butterflies and fish. Or you may buy a yellow tie with a nude on it, which in electric light becomes still more nude. (For the week-end, of course, you may buy a few odd bits, not quite so conservative as these.)

I must warn all my English readers that American laundries will surprise them. The laundries not only clean your shirts but your linen usually comes back in one piece and not in small instalments. Much pleasurable excitement is lost in that you may rest assured of finding the very same things in your laundry basket that you sent to the laundry. There is no pleasure and expectation in opening a laundry basket, as in England, where you so often find babies' napkins, women's night-gowns and Victorian panties with lots of lace, instead of your dull, unromantic shirts, pants and handkerchiefs.

Have the sleeves of your jacket pressed to a razor edge like the one you have on your trousers. Then, put a tremendous cigar in your mouth. The length of your cigar will be in proportion to your importance. The cigars of those belonging to the lower income brackets hardly exceed two or three feet. In the more modern American cars there is a round hole in the wind-screen so that the driver can stick his cigar through it. In the movie (a movie is in fact an ordinary cinema) you may burn the ears of people sitting in front of you without needing to say 'pardon me'.

Finally you buy a hat. American etiquette is extremely strict concerning hats. You must put on your hat before entering a room, whether in a public or private place. But you must not wear a hat in elevators (ordinary lifts) except in business premises, where you must. Whenever in doubt, leave it on. It is considered rude to take your hat off at any time during your honeymoon, in the bath and at the hairdressers.

WHEN you are dressed, start rushing. Where to does not matter—but rush somewhere, because everybody else is rushing all over the place. There are express lifts and express subway (that is to say underground) trains in America, there are places where you can have a four course lunch in 90 seconds and there are shipbuilding yards which produce two fifty thousand ton battle cruisers or liners every hour; babies, in the upper income bracket circles are produced in three months' time. The production of cheaper babies still takes a little longer.

The American grocer knows but little of the pleasures of an English shopkeeper who may discuss the weather with every single customer for three quarters of an hour on end, while a peaceful and understanding queue stands by, each one awaiting his turn for a friendly chat.

If you believe that London underground trains are crowded in rush hours, you are mistaken. At 9 A.M. or 5 P.M. on the Bakerloo Line between Piccadilly and Oxford Circus you will find a hermit-like solitude compared with a New York subway at the same period of the day. *There* people will placidly sit on your head and settle on your shoulders as pigeons do in the Piazza San Marco in Venice; elderly ladies will crawl about your knees and it is quite customary to find a few odd children in your pockets. When you think the coach is so crowded that it cannot possibly hold one single additional person, at the next station a group of seven cheerful youths will charge it, holding hands and rushing in a body from the requisite distance, till, by the kinetic energy generated, a few superfluous passengers are pushed out on the other side, through the closed doors and windows.

Nobody is angry or irritated. People enjoy themselves and smile kindly. They understand a guy who is in a hurry.

Homeward bound

They work in a hurry, talk in a hurry—in brief, staccato sentences—sleep in a hurry and even drink in a hurry, gulping down impatiently an amazing number of Manhattan cocktails, dry martinis or straight whiskies. They do not enjoy the drink itself, they drink with a purpose: they wish to become reasonably drunk within the shortest period of time possible.

Then you have to get accustomed to the size of things. The Empire State Building has 102 stories and Rockefeller Centre has more inhabitants—or rather more people working in it—than many large and famous cities in Europe. Texas is three times the area of the United Kingdom of Great Britain and Northern Ireland, although the United States itself is only the third largest country on the American Continent. The sugar bowl you find on your table there is a sky scraper in itself. You can see matchboxes which would put a smallish cabin-trunk to shame and each individual match would be quite suitable for use as fire wood in England. If you order southern fried chicken in a restaurant they give you so many pieces that you simply cannot believe it is not southern fried ostrich and you feel disgusted with yourself when you eat it all. The Sunday edition of a newspaper is not unlike a full set of the Encyclopaedia Britannica, and Coney Island has enough amusement places on top of one another, in a many miles long row, to keep a small Balkan country amused for seven years on end.

A friend of mine, a European painter, not long after his arrival in the United States did a portrait of the president of a huge chain store. The president liked the picture very much and asked how much it cost.

'Two hundred dollars,' my friend replied.

'Good'—the great man nodded. 'And how much would you charge if I ordered several copies?'

My friend was slightly offended but he needed money badly so he asked the president:

'It depends . . . How many copies would you need?'

'Five hundred.'

'I'm sorry . . . I did not quite catch the number.'

'Five hundred, I said. You see, I want my portrait to be hung up in all the offices of my company, all over the United States. But I will not pay you more than a hundred dollars apiece.'

This was more than the artist in my friend could stand:

'But excuse me, sir. . . . I am an artist and not a . . .'

'If you are an artist, do the job quickly,' snapped the great man and the bargain was struck.

That is how a European artist started his career in the United States. Now he specializes in presidents of chain stores and simply refuses to make portraits in less than two hundred copies. He is doing very well. A still life painted by him costs five hundred dollars but if you order a gross you get a twenty per cent reduction.

HOW TO GET GADGET MINDED

THE Americans are extremely gadget minded people and American gadgets have a peculiar characteristic: they work. On the Continent you used to walk up to an automat, drop in a coin, pull a handle and nothing happened. In America you can take a bet that you will get a piece of chocolate or chewing-gum for your cent. I have a streak of altruism in my nature, and personally I prefer the nonchalant Continental automats to the utilitarian American variety—but I admit that this is a matter of taste.

In an American kitchen you find an electric orange squeezer—for making orange juice—and a second mechanical one, just in case the electricity fails. (But electricity never fails.) You also find here an electric dish washer and a clothes washer, a refrigerator and a superb tin opener fixed on the wall; the gas can be lit without using a match or any other lighting device—by simply turning a handle; you will find a high pressure cooker in which you can cook a joint in ten minutes and any vegetable in two or three minutes. I had some cauliflower cooked that way and it really was exactly like the best cabbage I have ever tasted.

There is short shrift for bottles and containers. They have no value and are thrown away. The milk comes in paper bags, lard in jars, cheese in china dishes, flour in small linen bags, tomatoes in cellophane and salt is sold in shakers. These devices make the life of every housewife smooth and easy. They all wish, however, that one single additional device could be invented: domestic help. But that in most cases is quite out of the question.

English people are wise and conservative and strictly opposed to these gadgets which make life prosaic and over mechanised. How right they are, one has to admit, when one thinks of the dull, lifeless and uneventful way the

19

It works!

Americans heat their houses. Is there anything more exciting, inspiring and—should I say—manly than winter in England? The burst pipe is accepted as a phenomenon of the winter; you know that the pipes *will* burst one day but how exciting it is to spend first of all three pleasant days wrapping them up and then retiring to wait for D-day. How amusing it is to store the coal in a shed, in the garage or in the bath tub, to bring it up in buckets every day to the various rooms, to light fires in the open fireplaces, blow and wait and hold an open newspaper in front of you, swear and pray and do it again when it goes out. Then finally, when it works, the wind comes down the chimney and blows the smoke into the room and you have almost as much trouble in putting the fire out as you had in lighting it. But every day, of course, is not windy. There are cold but peaceful and lovely winter days when, at last, you can lie down on the floor facing your homely, friendly fire and enjoy a really good book; it is true that your hair may catch fire if you are careless but you will always have the consolation that your feet get frozen at the same time.

Modern Americans know nothing of these joys of living— they do not even know what they are missing. Their houses have oil heating; which means that a company fills up their tank with oil and all the owner of the house has to do is regulate a meter. This meter is a little clock: it is set to the required temperature—let us say 70°—and when the temperature rises to that point the heating apparatus stops working; if it falls to 69°, it starts up again. In addition to this, the clock can be fixed so that the heating is cut off automatically, let us say at 11 P.M., and restarted at 6 A.M. Poor people—the English reader will think with sympathy —what a dull life they must have! But perhaps . . . No, you are wrong again. The boiler does *not* get dirty and blocked and the whole system does *not* break down twice every year. The oil company, which sells the cheap heating material to you, keeps the boiler clean without any extra charge.

England, as a rule, is a rather warm but very draughty country; America is cold but well-heated. In fact, over-heated. On the coldest days, people sit in shirt-sleeves in front of the open windows. Not only the whole of Britain but the whole Continent could be nicely heated with the energy that escapes through the windows in the U.S.

There are automatic waiters in America, automatic parking police which call public attention to you if you park your car for longer than an hour; you can post your letter in a 'mailomat'—which stamps it for you; in restaurants photocell-doors open up automatically before waiters carrying heavy trays; there are automatic cloak-rooms, where you drop in a dime, get a key and close your own section of a steel cupboard. You can drop a dime in a machine which will photograph you, develop and print your picture and deliver it in a frame—all within sixty seconds; you can take out a life insurance policy from an automat and if you put a nickel in a juke-box and press a button, then all the customers in a restaurant have to listen to your favourite tune, maybe twenty times running, whether they like it or not.

I like the system of birthday telegrams, too. For a dollar, I believe, you may send a singing telegram, that is, the telegram boy will deliver it singing 'Happy birthday to you,' calling the addressee, for instance your grandmother, by her Christian name. For ten dollars a choir of ten delivers your telegram and for twenty five dollars the Postmaster General leads the choir.

Various new devices are now under construction:

(1) You push a button and fall in love.

(2) You pull a handle and get married.

(3) You pull a wire and get divorced.

(4) You turn a knob and you may consider yourself to have had a bath.

(5) All classical books to be equipped with a button. You may either read the book or push the button.

There are, however, two serious technical hitches in American life.

(1) A bus-driver is a most unhappy person. He has to do the following things: (a) collect money; (b) give change if required; (c) count the money and transfer it from his collecting box to another from which he can give change more easily; (d) open and close the automatic door; (e) keep a regular check on the number of passengers and his own timetable and (f)—I have almost forgotten this as he himself does occasionally—he has to drive the bus.

(2) In America you need two hands to post a letter. Every letter-box has a handle which you have to pull down; then you throw your letter in and release the handle. You can drive a car, stop a train or fly an aeroplane singlehanded, but you must use both hands to post a letter. If you have a parcel or a suitcase in one hand, you have to put it down to pull the handle.

Now, bus-drivers and letter-posters complain bitterly but American ingenuity has not yet found a way to alleviate their lot. I have two very original—I may even say revolutionary—ideas which may contribute to the solution of these problems. The possibility has occurred to me of employing a second man in the bus, who might perhaps be called the conductor—I think that would be a suitable name for him—who could deal with the passengers so that the driver could give his full attention to driving the bus. Secondly, I reasoned, why not dismantle all those little handles from the pillar-boxes, leaving them with their mouths permanently open so that letters could be thrown in without much strenuous physical effort? After all, the United States is a country of spectacular technical experiments and she may yet give a lead to the world even in this respect.

MANNERS

UNTIL an English or Continental child reaches the mature age of three, his mother cuts up his meat for him, pushes a fork into his right hand and tells him to eat it up. This is the way a well-mannered adult American behaves at table, uniting the parts of mother *and* child. First, he cuts up the meat for himself, then places his knife at the right side of his plate, takes the fork into his right hand and eats.

Table manners are usually quite senseless all the world over. The rules are created by a small class of people who ridicule others for eating differently. Any one class remains the ruling class of a society just as long as it can dictate the rules of handling the knife and fork. In Hungary, people started to bind their table napkins around their necks—in a ridiculous way, so that the table napkins should really protect their clothes—and that meant the end of feudalism in Hungary. In New Guinea a member of a cannibal tribe once cut the ears off a freshly roasted gentleman and—contrary to all tradition—offered them to the chief instead of the priest; next morning the supremacy of priests over the worldly chiefs was broken. In England there will be no serious social revolution as long as the working classes turn their fork upside down and shove their vegetables on top of it.

Table manners make little sense but they always have some reason for coming into existence. If someone took the trouble to psychoanalyse the American nation some interesting conclusions might be reached in the process of finding out why the people of the United States eat like babies of three years of age.

There is an important rule to remember about drinks. Americans have their coffee (always with cream) with the *entrée* and before the sweet (which is not called *sweet* in any case). At every meal you have to drink an immense amount of water, irrespective of whether you drink a dry martini, beer, wine and brandy as well. You swallow some food and immediately drink some water to wash it down. Village schools teach you that you must drink at least three glasses of water per meal; in high schools you are taught to drink at least five; Princeton, Yale and Harvard insist on twelve glasses as the absolute minimum. If you drink less than eight glasses you are considered a man of insufficient education.

But apart from these table rules, American manners are somewhat informal. Everybody is called by his or her Christian name. This is a very democratic habit. You may be called Sir John Soandso, D.S.O., Ph.D., LL.D., head of an important economic mission in the U.S. and anything else if you like, but you simply cannot stand on your dignity if you are introduced to people like this: 'This is John, this is Janet.'

If Mr Albert Einstein is interviewed in front of a microphone, the announcer will introduce him thus: 'Tonight we have in the studio Mr Albert Einstein, the famous scientific guy. Hiya, Albert, it's mighty nice to meet you. I want to ask you a few questions. First of all, Albie, what about relativity? Don't look so worried. Come on, Bertie, don't be shy.'

Friendliness is the general rule. If you are an elevator man and you want to enquire after the health of a tenant's wife, you hail him: 'Hiya Mister—how is the Missus today?' If you look a trifle downcast or worried, the bootblack will pat you on the shoulder and shout into your ear in an encouraging voice: 'Take it easy!'

'Hiya, Al!'

In conversation, you should show a certain human interest in your fellow men. After being introduced to someone, aim at finding out in the first five minutes what his profession is, how much money he makes, what his bank balance amounts to, whether he is faithful to his wife, the name, address, age and profession of his girl friend and whether he has ever cheated the income-tax authorities. When he asks you similar questions, answer frankly, and your open smile should encourage him to make further enquiries into your trade secrets, financial dealings and sex life.

Don't forget that listening to a low pitched voice is a strain on his ear, so shout, roar and howl as loudly as you can; remember on the other hand, that too much talking is a strain on his throat, so interrupt him frequently and save him the trouble of finishing his sentences.

State everything firmly and decisively and discourage contradiction. Do not use expressions like: 'I believe . . .,' ' I shouldn't think so . . .' These phrases are vague and unmanly. If you disagree with anybody's opinion, say bluntly: 'rubbish.' (Or 'garbage' as they call the rubbish in America.)

There is another important American habit you must take note of. The Americans are great letter writers. If you are invited to a party, you must write a letter to the hostess next day saying that you enjoyed her lovely party very much. Whatever happens in a family, you congratulate all the members. You congratulate people at Easter, Christmas and Whitsun. (By the way, the Americans have no bank holidays. Banks—surprising as it may seem—play no part whatever in *their* religious life.) You do not have to possess great literary talent yourself, because you can find printed cards for all possible occasions. In a stationery shop near

Wall Street I collected the following titles at random: Illness, Accidental Illness, Car Accidents, Hospital Illness, Patriotic Illness, Child Illness, Humorous Illness. (Naturally, I was curious to find out what 'Patriotic Illness' meant and was thrilled to find a beautiful card with the text: 'Get well to the tune of *Yankee Doodle Dandy*.' I have unfortunately lost my note about 'Humorous Illness', but as far as I remember, humorous illness is a kind of indisposition, at the end of which the patient makes a kick into the air in an extremely humorous way and then dies.) Furthermore: all sorts of combinations to sister and husband, son and wife, brother and wife, brother and uncle, daughter and husband, etc. I saw one section called 'Baby Thank You', with a special department for twin babies and sub-sections for two twin boys, two girls, and one boy and one girl. Finally there were Parting Cards with little pockets for money, to alleviate the sorrow of the person from whom you part.

While I was looking round, the shopkeeper walked up to me and asked:

'Can't you find the card you want, Kiddie?'

'No,' I replied. 'I want a greeting card to congratulate a great grandfather on the occasion of the birth of colour-blind triplets.'

'Sure'—he nodded seriously, picked out three cards from his stock, handed them to me and asked:

'Do you want it in English, Italian or Yiddish?'

HOW TO SPEND MONEY

ENGLISH people will find the American monetary system irritating and confusing. The English have their own simple system: twelve pence make a shilling, twenty shillings a pound, two shillings and sixpence make half a crown but a crown does not exist and two shillings make a florin but this expression is never used. You can explain the English system to any foreigner in five minutes and, if he is a person of extraordinary intelligence, after living two years in this country, he will know how much change he should get from half a crown if he has to pay one and eight.

A dollar, on the other hand, consists of a hundred cents and that's that. I explained to an American business man that the great advantage of the English system is hidden (and how well hidden it is!) in the fact that a pound may be divided into three equal parts—three times six and eight making exactly a pound. That may be very comforting, he replied, but he hardly ever wanted to divide a dollar into three equal parts; on the other hand if he makes a business deal with an English firm, he continued, and makes a profit, let us say, of ten per cent of £35. 17. 10 then he has to employ a specially trained book keeper for half a day to find out the exact amount of his earnings.

There is a complication with the names of the various American coins. A cent is called a penny (but the expressions halfpenny, twopence and threepence do not exist), a five cent piece is a nickel, a ten cent piece a dime, a 25 cent piece a quarter and a 50 cent piece is a half (to rhyme with chaff). A dollar is called a dull'r, the vowel being very long.

The prices of primary necessities are these: a subway ride and a telephone call cost a nickel each; a bus ride costs a

'Sorry, sir, there's no such thing as a one-guinea note!'

nickel, except in Fifth Avenue where it costs a dime; a shoe shine is a dime and *Reader's Digest* a quarter.

Prices are mysteries. The price of a pack (packet) of cigarettes is 18 cents in New York. You cross the Hudson River to the State of New Jersey where you pay much less for the same cigarettes; in Virginia you pay less again. On many articles you will find a price label. The figure means that the price of that particular article may be anything on earth, except the figure stated. I bought an overcoat in New York, marked $30. There was a sale on, however, and they charged only $24 for it. I handed over $24 to the shopkeeper but he laughed ironically in my face. I had to pay an additional $2.30 State Tax and 37 cents Federal Tax. In other words, the $30 coat cost $24, consequently I had to pay $26.67 for it.

People often put the question to me, whether life in New York is cheaper or more expensive than in London. New York is incomparably the most expensive town in the world, not because prices are so high but because you cannot resist buying anything and everything as long as you have a dime (see above) in your pocket.

If you are a particularly strong character and resist buying a pencil which is shaped like Miss Betty Grable's legs, then you will certainly fall for another with a telescope at the end. If you have just avoided the danger of purchasing a trumpet with a photograph of Mr Leopold Stokowski on it, you are almost sure to buy another trumpet in the next shop, which, when you blow into it, says 'Salami'. (It is remarkable how much funnier all these wonders appear in the shop than at home.)

I personally bought a great number of jackets and about half a dozen ball-point fountain pens. Thereupon I firmly decided to stop shopping because I had not too much money left. Next day, I saw a great number of multicoloured fountain pens (80 cents each), all turning around in a shop window, fixed to a red and blue wheel. If it had not been for the wheel, I should have passed the shop with a superior smile on my lips; as it happened, however, I could not resist temptation and bought two more pens. There was a little note attached to one reassuring me that this pen did not leak at a height of 15,000 feet and that I could write with it under water. As I do a considerable amount of writing under water, this was a pleasant surprise to me. I put the new pen in the pocket of my new jacket. The pen leaked. My new jacket was ruined, but as this happened not under water and only ten feet above sea level, the shopkeeper refused to accept responsibility.

SOON after your arrival in the United States, you will see on boards, envelopes and in the newspapers these words often repeated: New York, *N.Y.* . . . 'What does *N.Y.* stand for?' you will enquire. The answer is: New York. 'But you've said it once already, old boy,' you will object. 'We never say London *L.*, or Paris *P.*' You have, however, failed to grasp that the letters *N.Y.* mean that New York City is in New York State and not in Arkansas or Delaware, as the name would suggest. Of course, it is quite possible, even likely, that there are towns of the same name in two or even twenty two states, which is why, when writing down the name of a town or village, you have also to add the abbreviated name of the state, in which it is situated. These abbreviations drive you slightly mad. As long as you do not know the names of forty eight states, you are happy. You see the mysterious sign *Va* or *Ga* and do not care. Then you learn that *Va* stands for Virginia and *Ga* for Georgia and you think you have learnt something. Far from it. Many American states begin with the same letter. There are, for instance, three states beginning with *A*, three beginning with *C*, three with *I*, four with *W*, (not counting Washington D.C., which is not a state), eight beginning with *M* and eight with *N*.

There are certain abbreviations which are not too difficult to learn. I memorised, for example, fairly easily that *Ohio* stands for Ohio, *Iowa* for Iowa and *Utah* for Utah. These are skilful abbreviations which do not put too heavy a strain on a trained memory. You may guess with a certain amount of natural intelligence that *Ariz* indicates Arizona and *Calif* California. But then the *Mi-Mo-Ma* riddle comes in. When you see the sign *Mi*, you have no idea whether it stands for Michigan, Minnesota, Mississippi, or Missouri; you do not know whether the symbol *Ma* stands for Maine, Maryland or Massachusetts. You sigh with relief when you see the abbreviation *Mo*, because it is quite obvious that it can only stand for Montana. The fact that it really stands for Missouri is certainly not your fault.

CONTINENTAL and English people are very fond of old junk. I personally collect all sorts of letters, until they pile up in such a hopeless mess that I have to throw them away—usually together with my most important documents, as it is too much work to sort them out. My mother will never throw away a box. To save room she puts smaller boxes into larger ones and consequently she can never find anything she is looking for—but still, it is so nice to have those useful little boxes in the house. In many homes you will find an old trunk full of family pictures, old clothes, valuable lace and worthless combs, pins, pamphlets and theatre programmes.

Between the American and his material world there is a purely utilitarian relationship. They have the idea that an umbrella, for instance, is there to protect you against rain and not to be cherished as a souvenir. An Englishman will tell you proudly that his car is eleven years old and has done more than 80,000 miles; an American would be ashamed of this. He will, if he can afford it, exchange a perfectly good car for a new one every year. He would not even know the registration number of his automobile as he gets a new licence plate with a new number on it every year.

When it rains, people in America go into a shop and buy a pair of rubber overshoes for a dollar; when it stops raining, they step out of them, leaving the rubber shoes on the pavement. Even the garbage man will not collect them—for his own personal use, I mean. The same happens to umbrellas and if you buy a house, you are sure to find a lot of very good furniture and carpets in it (not included in the price, of course) because the former owner just would not take the trouble of removing them. Very often you see advertisements in the paper, announcing that if you are prepared to collect a piano at such and such an address, you may keep it.

The Americans discard whole cities in the same way. When a town has served its purpose—the gold rush is over, or a mine in the neighbourhood has been exhausted—they evacuate it, leaving houses and furniture behind. You can find a great number of ghost towns all over the place. There is no silly sentimentalism: 'Right or wrong, my own city'. If it is right—it is my own city; if it is wrong, I move to a better place.

The United States is certainly not a second hand country. They are not sentimental over old pants and old books. Occasionally they buy some antique stuff, provided it is in rather good condition and fairly new. Traditions? Their tradition is to have always the best, the most modern and most practical of everything. Grandfather clocks may chime midnight beautifully, usually at 25 minutes past 2 A.M.; *their* electric clocks are ugly, unromantic, have no history and no patina and they would be utterly useless but for the fact that they always show the right time.

HOW TO HAVE FUN

To be able to enjoy life in the United States, you must become kind-hearted and easy-going. The Americans are truly kind and good-tempered people, always ready to help others. Once, when I was using the 'mailomat'—the machine which stamps and posts your letters—at one of the railroad stations,* I dropped my dime into the slot reserved for pennies only. The machine did not work and a man walked up to me to ask what the matter was. I told him and urged him not to worry; I would drop another dime into the right slot and that would solve my problem. 'No, Sir,' he declared firmly and in two minutes about a dozen people —civilians and railwaymen and postmen—surrounded the machine, punching, pushing, beating, boxing, caressing, coaxing and kicking it, until it was cowed into submission and returned my dime. Then they showed me the right way to use the mailomat and my letter disappeared at the proper place, accompanied by the cheers and good wishes of the crowd. I thanked them for their help and remarked: 'It must be very interesting to see one's own letter stamped by this machine.' I merely wanted to make some conversation and nothing more brilliant occurred to me. 'Wait a minute, Sonnie,' said one of the postmen, which surprised me as I was wearing a beard in those days. The postman disappeared and returned a few seconds later with a key, opened the machine, looked for my letter and handed it to me very proudly. People are in a hurry, that is true; but they are always prepared to stop, help and please others. In England if you ask someone about a street, he will politely tell you where it is; or more likely, he will reply in a very civil tone that he is afraid he does not know. In America the person accosted may ask you why you want to get there. You will

* It was an ordinary railway station in fact

38

'I'm a stranger here meself'

tell him that you heard about an apartment (flat) which may be available there. Then he will accompany you to the address mentioned, will bargain with the landlord, hire the apartment for you, help to move in your heavier furniture and disappear before you have a chance of thanking him properly.

The primary purpose in life, for many millions of Americans is to 'have fun' or 'to have a kick out of life'. 'Having fun' is no complicated process. The movie is the greatest fun of all; dancing, playing cards, skating, or necking (kissing in a car with anybody, anywhere and at any time) is fun; looking at pictures in a magazine and drinking orange juice is also great fun. They are satisfied with everything and enjoy everything. To meet Mr Peter Lorre in the street is a real treat; to listen to an awful crooner in a second rate restaurant is a kick ; to witness a nice car accident is just too wonderful for words.

Years ago in London I knew a little English girl, called Eileen. She told me once: 'Me and my girl friend have such a wonderful sense of humour. We sit down and laugh for hours on end, without the slightest reason.'

I often thought of little Eileen in the United States of America.

NOT IDENTICAL . . .

IN Continental newspapers one can often see so-called 'not identical' notices. If a law-abiding citizen happens to have the same name as a criminal, he inserts a 'not identical' notice in the paper in order to avoid any misunderstanding. For example:

I, the undersigned John Horn, am not identical with Mr John Horn who was hanged this morning in the courtyard of Marko prison.

John Horn, hatmaker
23 Church Street

Often these notices refer not to criminals, but on the contrary, to honest, or sometimes even distinguished members of society. People are jealous of their identity and do not wish to be taken for anybody else. We all know that both Winston Churchill the writer and Winston Churchill the statesman were anxious to let the world know who is who and worked out an arrangement for signing their names differently.

I often thought of these 'not identical' notices while in America. I was personally held responsible for Britain's foreign policy, warned about the dangers of imperialism, told off for being anti-Russian and then reprimanded for being too much pro-Russian. I got into most serious trouble because of the British government's Palestine policy. People tried to persuade and convince me, threaten, cajole and beg of me; somebody declared most emphatically that the Jews and Arabs would understand one another like brothers but for the British who sow discord between them. An elderly gentleman drew me aside at a party, dragged me into another room, closed the door and besought me:

'Give it to the Jews.' I was so touched by his deep emotion and obvious sincerity that I was on the verge of giving it to the Jews, when I realised, at the very last moment, that I had to be firm.

I should like to take this opportunity of communicating the following announcement to all concerned:

I, the undersigned, am not identical with the Right Hon. Ernest Bevin, His Majesty's Secretary of State for Foreign Affairs.

George Mikes

II. MANHATTAN

THE CITY

MANHATTAN is, first of all, the name of a very popular cocktail. Secondly, it is the name of an island which forms the heart of New York N.Y. The island is thirteen miles long, two miles wide and lies at the mouth of the Hudson River. East of it runs the East River, which divides the island from Long Island. Manhattan covers 54·4 square miles and has a population of 1,889,924. It is also one of the five boroughs (or, as the Americans prefer to spell it, *boros*) of New York City and for the foreigner it *is* New York City. I do not intend to insult the population of the Bronx, Queens, Richmond and Brooklyn, but for the visitor New York N.Y. means skyscrapers, the Empire State Building, Rockefeller Center, tremendous traffic, dazzling neon advertisements, Central Park, Times Square, Harlem, the avenues and famous streets—and all these are to be found in Manhattan.

New York was first seen by an Italian navigator, Giovanni de Verrazano, in 1524. The city, originally called New Amsterdam, was a Dutch possession and it was the New Netherlands Company which was granted a charter for exclusive trading rights. The Dutch had considerable trouble with the administration of the new community, so the English with their customary readiness to help people in trouble, rid them of all their worries by taking the colony over by force in the seventeenth century. New Amsterdam was renamed New York. Manhattan island itself was purchased by the Dutch from Indians in 1626. It seems that estate prices were pretty low at that time.

New York is built in such a way that a great deal of amusement and fun, to which inhabitants of English towns are accustomed, is lost. Parallel streets were discovered in England in 1923 but most of the towns had already been built. An English town is not simply the communal dwelling place of a number of citizens, it is also an elaborate quiz; you cannot simply 'pass through' an English town, you have to solve it. Try to make a 'short cut' in an imperfectly known district, relying on your infallible sense of direction, and the Lord have mercy upon your soul! If you land in a *cul-de-sac* you are lucky; you are much more likely to find yourself in a cork screw street in which you twist and turn like a snake dancer until, fifteen minutes later, you are faced with the diverting task of extricating yourself from the utterly strange regions into which you have penetrated. Travellers like to thrill us with their tales about the difficulties and horrors of Himalayan exploration. I am not impressed. The Himalayas cannot possibly offer any problems until the English build a few carefully planned towns on them.

All this excitement and *joie de vivre* is lost in New York. Manhattan is full of parallel rows of buildings, those running from north to south being called avenues while those running from east to west are called streets.

The avenues and streets have only numbers instead of names. On the Continent streets are usually named after historic figures and politicians. Every twenty five years there is a revolution and a change of régime and then all the streets are re-christened and very often it is a criminal offence to call them by their former names. Sometimes even the postmen have no idea what the various streets in their district are called and occasionally people are not quite sure

Plus ça change, plus c'est la même chose

about the current names of the very streets they live in. These pleasures can never mean anything to the American. Régimes may come and go, the Republicans may take over from the Democrats and vice versa, new parties may gain or lose power, but 21st Street will keep its name under the most conservative or most revolutionary régime alike.

This is not the only disadvantage of the system. In London it may fall to your lot to find Alma Square N.W.8. You have a vague idea where it may be and ask seventy eight different persons and nobody knows exactly where Alma Square is. Bus-men who have driven past in its immediate neighbourhood for twenty eight years, have never heard of it. People who pass through it twice a day, only know that it is somewhere near, either in front of you or behind you, either to the left or—maybe—to the right. How nice it is to discover after two hours' research, just when you are about to give the whole thing up, that you have passed through Alma Square ten times during your tour, only

> (*a*) there are no new name placards, and (*b*) the old placards which say 'Wellesley Gardens' went out of date seven years ago and should have been utterly disregarded.

You feel a sense of triumph and superiority after finding Alma Square; but who on earth will feel a sense of triumph in New York on finding 79th Street between 78th and 80th Streets? Let the British build a town with numbered streets and *then* try to find 79th Street in it!

The English influence has, however, scored minor victories in New York. Broadway, for example, betrays every aspect of the independent British spirit. It has no number but a name; it is not at all straight, but it bends and curves and twists like a whimsical rattlesnake, all along the length of Manhattan. You walk uptown in Sixth Avenue and at 30th Street Broadway is to your right; you reach 40th Street and Broadway is to your left; at Central Park South it decides to take a sharp turn to the west and it passes the line of Eleventh Avenue, then still further up it turns back eastward again. You can play an exhilarating game of hide and seek with Broadway and always Broadway wins.

The English town planning spirit gained a few points around the Avenues, too. If you have numbers instead of names, the idea would be that Second Avenue should follow First, Third Avenue Second and so on. This belief is too naïve. Between Third and Fourth they succeeded in smuggling in a quite superfluous little avenue called Lexington. Half of Fourth Avenue is called Fourth Avenue, the upper part of it is called Park Avenue. Between Fourth and Fifth Avenues there is a further annoying phenomenon, named Madison Avenue, and then, between Fourth and Eleventh Avenues, Broadway. The Sixth Avenue as such has recently been abolished and renamed 'Avenue of the Americas'. Nobody ever speaks of the 'Avenue of the Americas', on the other hand no official sign acknowledges the fact that there is or ever was a Sixth Avenue. You will be directed by someone to walk along Sixth Avenue and you do not find Sixth Avenue; you find the Avenue of the Americas instead which, in turn, may not be shown on your map.

These oases of muddle are certainly appreciated by visitors from England. But all attempts at improvement are futile; New Yorkers have committed a basic error in planning Manhattan in such a logical way and all subsequent efforts, however noble, are wasted; Manhattan just missed its chance of becoming a second Soho.

THE Americans are a dynamic people. Consequently they prefer a dynamic muddle to a static muddle. In New York you may know indeed where you *are* but they have built a huge intricate subway system with the sole aim in view that you should not know how to get from where you are to any other place. The buses do auxiliary duties and as a neo-American friend declared to me: he had often been miscarried.

To travel by car would be comparatively easy, but nobody uses his car in New York, because so many people use it that traffic is congested and unbearably slow. So you try the bus.

I was accustomed to take a Number 4 at Pennsylvania Station and ride to Fifth Avenue. One day I discovered a Number 4 bus in Lexington Avenue and got in, but instead of arriving at Fifth Avenue I found myself somewhere in the Middle West. The driver laughed at me when I explained my case to him, because—he told me—I had taken a Lexington Avenue 4 instead of a Fifth Avenue 4. I learned later that they have many Number 4 buses in the town, so by skilful economy they save the use of several figures every year. These figures are given to charity at the end of the year, in one lump sum.

Next day I tried the subway. At Pennsylvania Station I boarded a subway train marked: 49th Street. That was exactly what I wanted. I started reading my newspaper and did not notice that at the next stop, at 42nd Street, all the passengers got out, leaving me alone in the whole train. The train started moving again but stopped in the tunnel and went on shunting up and down for about forty minutes. The conductor walked through the carriage three or four times, saw me there in my melancholy solitude but said nothing.

On his next appearance I asked him:

'When do we reach 49th Street?'

He laughed jovially:

'49th Street? But we ain't going to 49th Street. Why should we?'

'Excuse me, sir, I never suggested that you should if you don't feel like it. I only saw a board on this train saying that it *was* going to 49th Street and that gave me the foolish idea that it might be going to 49th Street. My fault, I admit.'

He became indignant.

'Everybody knows you got to change at 42nd.'

'I didn't know.'

'You didn't?' he said in an ironical tone. 'How long have you been living in New York?'

'Two days.'

'Two days,' he shouted triumphantly. 'Then you couldn't possibly have known.'

On another occasion, I asked the subway official at an 8th Avenue subway station how to get to Columbus Circle. 'Take the train here'—he smiled—'and get off at Columbus Circle.' I took the train there, reached 34th Street, then 42nd, then 50th and, as Columbus Circle is at 59th, I thought everything was mighty swell. Then some irregularities occurred. We reached a station called Seventh Avenue, then Fifth Avenue, then Lexington Avenue. Then we started moving again, did not stop for fifteen minutes and finally reached 23rd Street, Long Island City, which is on the eastern hemisphere. There I got out and told my story to an official. He found it entertaining and explained to me that I ought to have taken an *A* train instead of an *E* train, or an *E* train instead of an *A* train, or an *AA* train instead of an *FZ* train.

'But how could I have guessed that?' I asked him in despair.

'Everybody knows that,' he retorted with a superior smile on his lips and turned away from me with contempt in his heart.

All these closely guarded secrets would have been given away long ago had they not taken further security measures.

(1) In most cases they do not mark the various lines on which the stations lie. If they mark the line, they mark it in such a way that the boards should mislead the more naïve type of passenger. Seventh Avenue Subway is called Seventh Avenue Subway at one point but at the next station it is called I.R.T.-line. 'Everybody knows' that I.R.T. stands for Interboro' Rapid Transportation System (T meaning both Transportation and System), and this is just a colloquial name for the Seventh Avenue line. At 34th Street you will see B.M.T.-line and 8th and 6th Avenue trains are often called 'Ind Subway', meaning Independent Subway which is just a cute way of telling the public that the line is not independent, because all subway lines belong to the city.

(2) Subway maps are as closely guarded as military secrets. You cannot find a subway map at any station. You can find maps *inside* the carriages and there you can find out which subway you should have boarded instead of the one you actually did board. Those maps, too, show only that particular line on which you are travelling and if you want to change, you are absolutely free to choose a new line, wherever and whenever you wish.

In the New York subway system there are parallel tracks for local trains and express trains. The local train stops at every station, the express only at every fifth or sixth station. I always travelled by express. If I do not know in any case —I reasoned—where I shall arrive, at least I wish to arrive there as quickly as possible.

HOW TO BE SNOBBISH

Many Americans dislike the English because—they say
—the English have an uppish and superior attitude towards
the rest of humanity. The English have not created a civilisation in the sense that ancient Greece and Renaissance Italy
did, but, as it happens, they have been the flag-bearers of
modern Western civilisation for the last few decades.
They carry that flag as a well-disciplined country gentleman
carries an umbrella; they do not wave it about, extolling its
merits, they just open it in rainy weather and carry it
calmly, protecting themselves first of all and then anybody
else who cares to get under it; they smile in amusement at
those strange fellows who rush around bewildered and bare-
footed in the rain but pass no remark on them.

That umbrella would be somewhat less unbearable if it
were not so black. If only they painted a few red and blue
circles on it and an occasional nude in yellow.

In America this superior attitude is quite unknown. Nobody looks down upon anybody; all men and women are
considered equal with the following exceptions:

There are a great number of people of Anglo-Saxon
descent who look down upon the rest of the community.
The ancestors of these people came over in the *Mayflower*.
One of these *Mayflower* people once boasted to a refugee
about his ancient roots in America, upon which the refugee
retorted: 'But *I* came here when there was already a strict
immigration control in force.' Another person once remarked: 'My ancestors came over in the *Mayflower*.' To
which another replied: 'And my ancestors were on the re-
ception committee.' (He was an Indian.)

The *Mayflower*, by the way, was a vast ship of 85,000 tons
and made innumerable trips between Southampton and

'Pleased to meet you!'

Plymouth (New England): that is how so many people crossed in her.

Furthermore all white people look down upon Mulattoes;

all Mulattoes look down upon Negroes;

all Negroes look down upon Mulattoes;

all people of Scandinavian origin look down upon Germans;

all Germans look down upon Central Europeans;

all Central Europeans look down upon Italians, Spaniards, Armenians and Persians;

all Italians and Spaniards look down upon Central Europeans and Irish;

all of them look down upon Jews;

all Jews look down upon everybody else;

all Americans look down upon New Yorkers;

all New Yorkers look down upon Mid-Westerners and Wild-Westerners;

all Northern people look down upon Southerners;

all Southerners look down upon the 'Yanks'.

All emigrants look down upon the refugees (an emigrant is a refugee who arrived before 1933, a refugee is an emigrant who arrived after that date). All refugees look down upon those who arrived in a later ship and if people came in the same ship those who got off first look down upon the newcomers whose luggage was examined a little later.

All those who are 'citizens' look down upon those who have only just got their 'first papers'. Those with their first papers look down upon the pseudo-visitors who are trying to settle in the United States.

It is easy to see that the people looked down upon most by others in the United States are Yiddish speaking Negro Jewish refugees with expired visitors' visas.

NEW York is the second largest city in the world. New York is a provincial town; it is not the capital of the United States and not even the capital of New York State.

In our eyes New York is a solid American city. Writers have tried to define a 'nation' on racial, historical and economic grounds—and failed mostly because the United States and Switzerland defy all definition. I believe it is fair to say that a nation consists of people who read the same newspapers, listen to the same radio programme, play the same games and hold their knife and fork in the same way. In that sense New York is a hundred per cent American. At the same time more Britishers live in New York than in Brighton or Birkenhead, almost as many Irish as in Dublin, more Germans than in Cologne, more Poles than in Cracow, more Austrians than in Salzburg, as many Hungarians as in Szeged, more Russians than in Kiev, more Italians than in Naples, more Negroes than in South West Africa and more than five times as many Jews as in Palestine.

An American and a New York way of life is superimposed on the whole community but underneath it, or parallel with it, the various communities live their own lives and everybody seems to be proud of his origin. The day following my arrival in New York, I went for a walk in Chinatown, entered a shop, and there was a dairyman, sitting chatting with the Chinese proprietrix. He started talking to me in that outspoken and straightforward American fashion:

'Are you Jewish? Because you look Jewish.'

Then he looked at me again and declared:

'No, you don't look Jewish, but you look like a refugee.'

'Thank you,' I nodded with appreciation.

'You are dressed like a refugee.'

'No doubt.' (I had my best English suit on.)

'No offence meant.'

'No offence taken.'

'I am Jewish myself.'

'Are you?'—I exclaimed with surprise.

'Sure.   And I am proud of it.'

I turned to the Chinese woman but before I had an opportunity of telling her what I wanted, the dairyman continued the conversation.

'What are you?'

'I am proud, too.'

'I mean it. What are you?'

'I am a Polish Negro.'

'But you are white.'

'Yeah. Not so white as you think.'

'White enough.'

'Didn't you know? In Europe Negroes *are* white.'

He would not take it.

'You're kidding. When did you arrive here?'

'Yesterday.'

'Only yesterday? But you speak very good English.'

'I've been living in London.'

'In London? Do they speak English there, too?'

'Kinda English,' I declared firmly and the conversation was closed.

All these national communities are settled in separate districts. In Yorkville you see German boards on the shops with German names on them, German newspapers are sold in the streets, German films are shown in the cinema and you may walk up to anybody, address him in German and the chances are nine to one that he would reply in German.

Big chain stores in this district would not employ an assistant if he did not speak German fluently. The same description applies to any other national district and if you turn the dial on your radio slowly around, you are certain to hear commercials sung in Yiddish and Spanish, in Swedish and Armenian and scores of other European and Asiatic languages. There are craftsmen of so many nationalities in New York that you can get anything on earth in the shops and restaurants. Rumanian peasant dresses, Venetian glass, Marseilles bouillabaisse, Italian salami, Pilsen beer, Chinese back scratchers—and all a shade better than the original.

In most cases the children of these people learn the American language perfectly but sometimes they speak only their ancestors' mother tongue even unto the second or third generation. You find people seventy five years old, who were born in New York, never left the city boundaries and who speak only Ukrainian or Schwitzerdeutsch. Occasionally rather unexpected things occur. Three years ago my brother, then still in uniform, was driving through Brunswick, New Jersey—a town with a large Hungarian population. Having lost his way, he stopped in front of a house and asked a little Negro boy, in English, how he could reach the main road. The boy turned away, opened the gate and shouted to his mother in Hungarian, with a broad Transdanubian accent: 'Mother, come quick, there is a soldier here.'

All these people are or will become citizens. It is true, they always retain a certain interest in their country of origin, but their loyalty to the United States is unquestionable.

Luckily there is no patriotism of the sort one saw, for instance, in pre-war Italy. I never heard or read a word about 'our beloved, sacred country'. Every now and then they speak of the American flag and they all adore the 'American way of life'—which in their eyes seems to be a matter of honour; in ours it is a matter of taste. They are all grateful to the country which gave them freedom and grapefruit, a high standard of living and the comic strips in the newspapers, employment and chewing-gum, Abraham Lincoln and Frank Sinatra. They are all citizens, except the 333,000 Indians, who I believe are considered visitors.

Abraham, son of Kentucky

IN America, just as in England, you see the same shops with the same boards and windows in every town and village.

Shopping, however, is an art of its own and you have to learn slowly where to buy various things. If you are hungry, you go to the chemist's. A chemist's shop is called a drug-store in the United States; it is a national institution and a very good institution at that. In the larger drug-stores you may be able to get drugs, too, but their main business con-sists in selling stationery, candy, toys, braces, belts, fountain pens, furniture and imitation jewellery. Every drug-store has a food counter with high stools in front of it and there they serve various juices, coffee, sundaes, ice cream, sand-wiches, omelettes and other egg dishes. A friend of mine in Hollywood met Otto Hapsburg, the claimant to the Austrian-Hungarian throne, who—I understand—apart from his hobby of calling himself a king, is an extremely charming and cultured young man. My friend called on Otto one morning in his hotel. He was received by the *aide-de-camp* who declared ceremoniously:

'*Seine Majestät nimmt sein Frühstück in der Apotheke.*' (His Majesty is having his breakfast in the pharmacy.)

If you want cigarettes, go to the grocer; if you want to have your shoes cleaned, go to the barber; if you want a radio, go to a man's shop; if you want a suitcase, go to the chemist's. On the other hand if you want to send a tele-gram, avoid the post office, because telegrams are handled by private companies. Nor has the post office anything to do with the telephone either, as telephone service is supplied by the American Telephone and Telegraph Co. Nor will you find public conveniences in America in the British sense of the word because a lavatory is a strictly private enterprise in the United States.

Whatever you buy, it may be exchanged later for something in the same shop. This is a great pastime with the Americans. A great many people do not really buy things —they only acquire some raw material for later exchanges. It is not unusual at all to see a lady bringing back a hat with a lot of fruit on it and exchanging it either for real fruit or a real hat; or to see somebody bringing back a refrigerator with the remark that he made a mistake and now he wants to subscribe to the *Reader's Digest* instead.

You do not need to time your shopping very carefully because you will find some shops stay open in New York all night. The big department stores keep open till 9 P.M. once a week. Should you want a meal at any time of the day or night, that is quite easy. If you have a party in your house and you decide at 2.30 A.M. to have some music, you can rush down to the corner, buy a piano and it will be delivered to your home within half an hour. If you fancy playing golf at 3.45 in the morning you can purchase, if you wish, a set of golf clubs and balls. I still cannot quite decide what to do with that Indian feather head-dress I bought one morning at 5.15 in Greenwich Village, but I was deeply impressed by the tempting opportunity and could not resist buying it.

You must be extremely careful concerning the names of certain articles. If you ask for suspenders in a man's shop, you receive a pair of braces, if you ask for a pair of pants, you receive a pair of trousers and should you ask for a pair of braces, you receive a queer look.

I should like to mention that although a lift is called an elevator in the United States, when hitch-hiking, you do not ask for an elevator, you ask for a lift.

There is some confusion about the word *flat*. A flat in America is called an apartment; what *they* call a flat is a puncture in your tyre (or as they spell it, *tire*). Consequently the notice: FLATS FIXED does not indicate an estate agent where they are going to fix you up with a flat, but a garage where they are equipped to mend a puncture. Only once did I see this popular notice, FLATS FIXED, on a shop which sold brassières. The customary slogan for these establishments is: 'United we stand, divided we fall'.

An average English motorcar could be placed, I believe, without much difficulty, in the luggage-rack of an average American automobile. A well-known, but rather small English 8 h.p. car is on show in a window in 42nd Street and is exceedingly popular with the entire population. There is always a huge crowd in front of the shop window and everybody is roaring with laughter. 42nd Street is the movie street in New York and if people cannot get into the cinema, they spend an hour or two in front of that shop window and consider their excursion well worth while.

'Seeing the car' is a regular item of all sight-seeing tours, too. I was deeply hurt when a veteran who had served in England explained to his friends:

'These little things, you know, have to run on the *roads* in England. I think it's very unfair. They should not be allowed to get off the pavement.'

I talked to an English motorcar expert over there, who had something to do with that show too, and asked him, who on earth bought these cars in the United States, considering that they are not cheaper than a 30 h.p. Chevrolet.

'They are moderately popular in the country.'

'In the country of Great Britain and Northern Ireland you mean?' I enquired.

'No, I mean here in the various States. In Oregon, for instance, they are very much appreciated.'

'I see . . . That is why you exhibit them in New York. A jolly good idea, particularly if you come to think of the fact that New York is practically as far from Oregon as it is from London.'

'That is a good point,' he nodded. 'A very good point indeed. Distances *are* amazing in this country, aren't they?'

In the United States the price of steel is much lower than in Britain, mass production methods are much cheaper, petrol is very much cheaper (which is important because the consumption of these huge cars is very high) and there is no horse-power tax. One has to pay a certain amount according to the weight of the car for one's licence plate every year—that is all.

An American car is as big as a railway engine. There is a radio set in every car, cigar lighter, electric heater, air conditioner, a set of openly placed and hidden lights, nylon seat covers, electrically operated windows and convertible seats which may be used as beds. Now they are experimenting with a view to introducing running hot and cold water, baths and a foot-bath for the driver for hot days, an elevator and a crane to save passengers from the fatigue of using their own feet when getting in and out. In spite of all these devices and gadgets, they still find a cute way of placing the engine somewhere. These motors are terrific—in New York and other big towns they are able to crawl at a speed of eight miles per hour without much trouble and in fact no speed is too slow for them. It is much more difficult on the highways where real skill, energy and determination is needed to keep a low speed. There are only fifteen states where you may drive faster than 50 m.p.h., at no single point in any state is the speed limit removed and in Washington D.C. you must not exceed 25 m.p.h. Still it is fun thinking how fast you *could* go in these modern marvels, if only you could go fast.

Modern American cars have no starter, or to put it more clearly, the starter is built together with the gas-pedals. You turn the ignition key, push the gas-pedal down and the

C

motor starts. And it *does* start, mind you. An American friend asked me whether I still had a starter on my English car.

'Oh no. . . . No starter on my car . . .' I replied and changed the subject.

This was the truth but not the whole truth. The whole truth is that my starter broke about a year ago and was removed and now I always have to use the handle when I want to start the car. No starter—no starter. You may use different means for achieving the same end.

The forty eight states of America have varying laws relating to motor vehicles, which fact does not make the motorist's life any happier. In Alabama you have to apply for a new licence plate on October 1. In Ohio on March 1, in New York on January 1 and in California on January 2. In Louisiana you may start driving at the age of fourteen, in Vermont you must be at least eighteen. Driving tests differ everywhere and in three States no driving licence is required at all. In some states you may stay for ninety days with your home licence plate, in others only for twenty five. But these are only minor difficulties. The real trouble arises when, driving through a 'foreign' state you make a U-turn, for instance. (A U-turn is a full turn in a street.) In some streets you are only supposed to make a Y-turn. (A Y-turn is a turn where you shuttle backwards and forwards and this expression does not exist at all—but I feel it should exist.) Then you may be put in jail on a Saturday afternoon and kept there until Monday morning on the excuse that the sheriff is away for the week-end, or too busy to deal with your case. On Monday morning, as a rule, you have the choice of paying one, twenty, fifty or a hundred dollars fine

The girl who took the wrong turning

or of waiting for the decision of a higher court, the only difficulty being that you have to wait for it in jail. A friend of mine just rushed down in Atlanta, Georgia, to buy a couple of aspirins for his wife at 3.14 P.M. on a Saturday and returned at 11.17 A.M. on Monday without the aspirins, having spent all his money on an expensive but not very entertaining U-turn.

To fine 'foreign' motorists is not only an exciting pastime but a safe and permanent income for certain towns and many people are quite prepared to make a forty or fifty mile detour to avoid a certain city because they know that the sheriff there is fond of unusually long week-ends. I met one gentleman who bought an aeroplane and flies to his office every morning from a nearby town because the air, for the time being at any rate, is free of troopers—i.e. state traffic police.

The American roads are the best in the world. Wide, safe highways cut across the big cities and the whole country and there are no traffic lights and no cross-roads anywhere. Cross-roads run either above or underneath the highways and side-tracks always lead up or down to them.

Parking is perhaps even more difficult in New York than it is in London. The police used to be bullied in both cities because parking cars blocked so many roads. One ingenious New York police official found a solution to this problem and forbade parking in a number of streets. This example was readily and swiftly followed in London. Now people know they must not park in certain streets. But where should they park? The police shrug their shoulders. There is plenty of space on the moon. In New York, even garages are full, but it is strictly forbidden to keep a car in the street overnight. Garages, however, when they cannot find room for all the cars on their premises, *are* allowed to keep cars in the street. So this situation has arisen: you pay the garage a high fee to have your car under shelter during the night, in return for which fee, you may keep it in the street.

IT was decided almost two hundred years ago that English should be the language spoken in the United States. It is not known, however, why this decision has not been carried out.

Dictionary
of the
American
Language

HOW TO GO BANKRUPT

IF you feel like going bankrupt, do not hesitate to do so. There is no stigma, or even blame attached to it. It is true that success is the measure of what you are worth; but you cannot achieve success without trying hard and it is obvious to every American that a number of experiments are bound to fail. The foundation of American commercial life is credit. It is easy to obtain credit. It is easy to open—let us say—a modern barber's shop with seventy five chairs, equipped with hair drying, hair washing and massage machines, X-ray and ultra-violet apparatus and with a huge surgery where one or two barbers (who are not very good at shaving) remove tonsils and appendices much cheaper than the neighbouring hospital. Yes, it is easy to open such an establishment on credit but you must pay the instalments or you are lost.

But you are not 'lost' in the English or Continental sense. On the Continent, ruin means ruin; the possibilities are extremely limited. All the people in a certain branch of business know one another or at least know of one another and there is little chance of recuperating, or at any rate, it needs exceptional energy, perseverance and doggedness. In England again, it is the moral side of the question that is so difficult to bear. A person who is unable to meet his liabilities, in most cases feels a fallen man. In plutocratic America, money means money—openly and brazenly; in England, money, for a newly grown up and incurably snobbish middle-class, means social status and when bankruptcy brings home the harsh fact that this social status was based primarily or exclusively on money—that, usually, has a crushing moral effect. For the American, a temporary and transitory status of bankruptcy does not mean more than a 'nasty morning' means for the English. It is nasty today, it will probably be nasty tomorrow and the day after tomorrow but a week today—well, we shall see. . . . Commercial life on the whole is just as scrupulously honest in the United States as it is in Britain. But every moneylending firm is prepared for a certain percentage of loss. If the proprietor of the barber shop cannot pay the instalments, the shining, silvery machines will be dismantled, the X-ray and ultra-violet apparatus wrapped up carefully and carried away and the surgery delivered to the neighbouring hospital. The ex-barber smiles and takes it easy. For a few months perhaps he will sell ice cream in the street, clean shoes or take a job as a radio commentator on international affairs and then he tries again—this time manufacturing honey (sold in tubes), or fertilisers or producing a psycho-analytical magazine. I do not intend to convey the idea that every rich American becomes bankrupt twice every year; but this sort of thing certainly occurs periodically to a great number of people.

A person may have been working in an office for 37 years and then one Saturday he may be informed by the boss that his services are not required any more and he should not take the trouble to come in on Monday next. The question of notice, let alone pension, does not arise. Or a person who may have flourished as a toothpaste manufacturer for two decades, may find himself one day busily trying to found a little firm in order to export children's underwear to Chile.

America is called a country of unlimited possibilities. We have heard so many stories of the little boot-black who finished his life as a good, wise, multi-millionaire steel manufacturer, newspaper magnate or refrigerator king. It is rarely mentioned that there is a two-way traffic on these

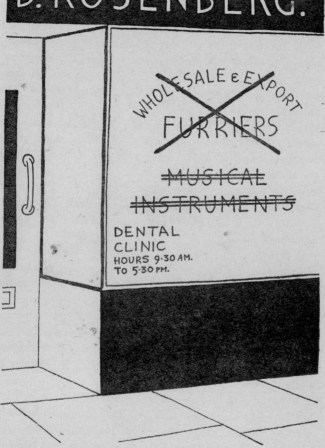

A Rosenberg by any other name . . .

roads of unlimited possibility, and the amazing career of the youthful multi-millionaire who starts his life as a newspaper magnate or refrigerator king and ends it as a good, wise, elderly boot-black—has still to be recorded.

HOW TO DIE

IT is great fun dying in the United States of America. It is great fun first of all for the undertakers who make a wonderful living out of it but also for the deceased who suddenly becomes the centre of attention and fuss.

American newspapers are full of funeral advertisements:
'Funeral Service that will leave your mind at ease for ever.' Or:
'A Funeral Service you will really enjoy.' Or:
'Dignified funeral.' Or:
'Comfortable funerals.' Or:
'Funeral that will make your family happy for months.' Or:
'Unforgettable funerals as low as $150. The same with southern plants $200. The same with two palms $215.' Or:
'Funerals with hidden neon lighting from Louis XIV rooms.' Or:
'Come to us! We'll bury you better!'

And people go. They discuss their own funerals with gusto, choose the coffin (first their measurements are taken for this purpose), choose the decorations on it, the songs to be sung, the palms to be exhibited, how they are going to be embalmed. They pay in instalments and look forward to the great day.

I do not wish to go into all the details of this morbid but flourishing industry although there is something fascinating in the gaiety of the undertakers. They are the only business-men in the world who can look upon everybody on earth as prospective customers. They look at old men with a re-proachful eye and with sanctimoniously hidden self-assur-ance and, at the same time, one can see the hope shining in

'*Why, Elmer, it's perfect!*'

their eyes that they will order it with southern plants and two palms.

It is worth pointing out that dishwashing is not the only occupation a man without much skill and expert knowledge can undertake, when absolutely broke. You can always become a professional mourner. The undertaker will pay you 25 per cent and his price list is this:

> You stand by the coffin with head bent and looking very sad—five dollars.
>
> The same with occasional tears—ten dollars.
>
> The same with crying, shrieking and sobbing—twenty-five dollars.
>
> For seventy five dollars you have to throw yourself into the grave after the coffin.

Orders of this kind, however, have recently decreased. (Because the price is considered unreasonably high.)

ADVERTISEMENTS

I AM ready to bet that in your *naïveté* you believe that advertising is the art of convincing people of the remarkable qualities of your wares; of persuading them to prefer your product to any other make; and of keeping certain brands permanently in the public eye.

This is a misconception. Advertising—as I read somewhere—is the art of convincing people that they want certain things they do not want at all; of making them dissatisfied with everything they have; of making them thoroughly unhappy.

Advertisements in America are ubiquitous. They fill the newspapers and cover the walls, they are on menu cards and in your daily post, on pamphlets and on match boxes, they are shouted through loud speakers and shown in the cinemas, flashed electrically and written on the sky by aeroplanes and whispered in front of your window while you sleep so that you should dream of tooth paste, shoe polishes and soap flakes.

Leaving the problem of 'commercials'—i.e. the spoken and sung radio advertisements—for the moment, I find that there are five main ways of making people particularly unhappy.

(1) *Repetition.* If you hear these five letters: L.S.M.F.T. for the first time in your life, you remain cool and unimpressed. L.S.M.F.T. *Lucky Strike Means Fine Tobacco.* 'And what then?' you say. It is not funny, it is not witty, in fact, it is simple, silly and flat. Then you try to find the President's latest speech in the newspaper, but you cannot find it. You find these five letters instead: L.S.M.F.T. You travel on the subway and try to think of a killing reply to an important and annoying letter you have received but you cannot think of anything, because wherever you look you see only five letters: L.S.M.F.T. You take a walk in a dark street in comparative solitude, thinking of your beloved, and suddenly a neon advertisement flashes into your eyes: L.S.M.F.T. You want to write a poem on the uselessness and vanity of worldly pleasures but you only write down fifty times: *Lucky Strike Means Fine Tobacco*. If you try to recite the alphabet you are sure to slip up: g, h, i, j, k, l, s, m, f, t. . . . At this stage the advertisement has achieved its purpose. You will then and there take a solemn oath that whatever should happen in the future, however long you may live, you would rather go without smoking altogether than put one single Lucky Strike into your mouth.

(2) *Logical conclusions*. Advertisements have a special logic of their own. They tell you by implication that if you use a certain orange squeezer in your kitchen, you remain young, lovely and beautiful; if you wash with a certain soap you become rich; if you wear a certain type of underwear you inherit a large sum from a wealthy uncle and if you use only a special kind of tomato ketchup you learn foreign languages more easily. Of course, people are much too intelligent to believe such silly statements. But as after all there may be *something* in it—why not try? And as people who inherit large sums from wealthy uncles usually do wear some type of underwear and a few others who insist on a certain kind of tomato ketchup do learn French with the greatest ease, the proof is soon to be found that the advertisements—amazing as it may seem —spoke the golden truth.

Inheritance

(3) *The semi-scientific approach.* The word: 'scientific' has a magic effect in America. You may put up a notice: 'Scalp massage': this is quite ineffective. But if you say: 'Scientific scalp massage'—that is a different matter. After all, the least you can expect is that your scalp should be massaged by a scientist. A shoe polish manufacturer invented the verb: *to lanolize.* Other shoe polishes just clean your shoes—nicely, cleanly, efficiently—but E. shoe polish lanolizes them. The word has no meaning whatever but it is quite obvious that everybody would much rather have his shoes lanolized than merely cleaned. I am a rather lazy shoe lanolizer but I just could not resist the temptation. If you have 50,000 dollars to spend, you can persuade people that while other tooth pastes just clean their teeth, Atlantis tooth paste saturnizes them; that any other soap just washes their clothes but Atlantis soap kepplerizes them. And all good people in America would much rather spend their time lanolizing, saturnizing, kepplerizing, constricating, saharizing, tripodizing and patagonizing than washing and cleaning, because washing and cleaning, after all, *are* rather dull.

The other approach on the same line is to give people statistics. You state, for instance, that Amalda floor polish gives 42 per cent more shine to the floor with 37 per cent less effort than any other make. If anybody questions your statement and declares that its stupidity is too obvious for any child over the age of four, you smile in a superior way and explain to him that this has been 'scientifically' proved. If he is still unconvinced, tell him that the real explanation lies in the fact that any other floor polish just cleans the floor but Amalda platonizes it.

(4) *Glorify your weakness*. There was a chewing-gum firm in New York which used only artificial flavours instead of real fruit flavours. This fact became known to the public and sales dropped off. Then suddenly huge advertisements appeared: 'X—the only chewing-gum made with real ARTIFICIAL flavor.'* People's imagination was caught and few would look at any other chewing-gum now.

(5) *Religion*. Religion has recently become extremely popular. In the advertising field, I mean. Churches advertise, too, ('Come to us and you will be not only saved but amnetized!') but this is not the real point. Religion has immense possibilities. I print here a little article, published in one of the American newspapers while I was over there. No comment is needed, I believe:

> Last week company-president Maurice C. Smith Jr hired the Reverend Dale D. Dutton away from a wealthy Baptist Church to make him Bristol Shoe's vice-president of Christian relations. The job: 'To do good as he is led to do it.' The budget: $100,000 p.a. The inspiration: 'His instructions will come not from the company but from God. . . . We do not expect to sell any more shoes because of this venture.'

If the sales fall off, spend more money on advertising. But beware of one thing: do *not* improve the quality of

* They really mean flavour

your goods. That will leave you a smaller sum to spend on advertising—and then you are lanolized. Maybe you are lanolized for good.

THE EMPIRE OF SOAP OPERAS

'Every country has the radio service it deserves.' To apply this axiom to the United States of America would be a grave insult and I hasten to add that the United States deserve something much better than the radio service it has. American radio is the reverse of the Shakespearean stage. In Shakespeare's time the world's greatest dramas were acted with the most primitive technical arrangements; on the American air the world's most primitive writing is performed under perfect technical conditions.

There are four major radio networks: ABC (American Broadcasting Corporation, four stations and 215 affiliated stations); CBS (Columbia Broadcasting System, seven stations, 157 affiliated stations and 123 Latin American stations); MBS (Mutual Broadcasting System, 329 affiliated stations); and NBC (National Broadcasting Company, six stations, 153 affiliated stations and 162 Latin American stations). In addition to the network there are innumerable local stations—broadcasting in many languages but mostly in English—and a number of them are very important and influential. A local New York, Chicago or Los Angeles station, after all, has several million potential listeners.

Licences for broadcasting stations (for receivers no licences are needed) are issued by the Federal Communications Commission which body is supposed to coordinate and, to some extent, control the work of all stations. Some time ago FCC sharply criticised the 'broadcast licensees' and the result was a tremendous uproar on the licensees' part because they considered that 'freedom of speech' was endangered. Whenever a big commercial trust is criticised or its rights curtailed it cries out that some fundamental human right is in peril.

The main features of American broadcasting are these:

(1) Radio is a permanent background noise in America. All the radios of the land seem to be switched on all the time, and considering that 34·6 per cent of the population own radio sets compared with 18·8 per cent in the United Kingdom, you may guess that they are capable of a considerable din. In apartments, in the street, in shops, restaurants, cars and taxis, anywhere and everywhere the noise goes on—it is your fate to listen to it, whether you like it or hate it.

(2) Public opinion, taste and culture are led and directed by laxative, cigarette, soap and cheese companies. They buy a certain amount of time on the radio, during which they try to convince you that *their* laxative is tastier, more efficient, cheaper and more beautiful to look at than any other laxative in the world. To fill up time between two commercials, they hire some comedians who crack a number of stale jokes and laugh at them themselves, loudly and heartily. Of course, Mr Bob Hope or Mr Morgan and a few others *are* funny and amuse you most of the time, but they are very rare exceptions.

This system was hailed as the real freedom. No state control, they boasted, no censorship. Some keen observers, however, noticed after the lapse of a few years that the real aim of laxative firms was not to raise the cultural standard of the nation but to sell more laxatives to people whether they needed them or not. In this they have succeeded; and the result is American broadcasting.

(3) Everybody and everything is 'Hooperated'. All radio performers and writers depend on Mr C. E.

Believe it or not

Hooper's fortnightly *Hooper Ratings*. Hooper speaks on behalf of thirty five million American radio families, makes $1,000,000 p.a. and has nearly two thousand employees who ring up people, trying to find out what they listen to. Mr Hooper tells in his *Ratings* what per cent of radio fans listen to a certain programme. America is a scientific country. Mr Hooper's assistants ring up people day and night, collect answers to relevant and irrelevant questions put in a skilful or clumsy way, issue statistics by the score and state extremely scientifically indeed that a song called *Open the Door Richard* is 137 times more popular than Beethoven's *Fifth Symphony* and Mr Ovington's chats on 'How I like my cheese and why' are 217·08 times better liked than *A Midsummer Night's Dream*.

(4) A special feature in American broadcasting is the soap opera. Once upon a time, very few people listened in around noon and then a soap company hit on the idea that special broadcasts should be initiated for women who are at home preparing lunch. So the soap operas started their career and now practically all stations broadcast these soap operas between 12 noon and 4 P.M. on every weekday from Monday to Friday. They last fifteen minutes each. One of the most popular is the *Romance of Helen Trent*. Miss Trent is just an average American girl. She has been thirty two for the last two decades; she is intelligent, beautiful and employed as a designer by one of the Hollywood film companies and in spite of the fact that she is begged and besought twice every week to become a film star she refuses and remains just that little, unassuming average American girl she has never been.

She solves life's problems for anyone who happens to come near her or pass down the street in front of her window. These are usually grave and momentous problems. There is for example a young man who has charming manners and an admirable character, is a graduate of Princeton University, has an income of four million dollars per year, loves Helen Trent's colleague madly; she loves him, too, and their parents agree to the marriage—what are they to do? Everybody is at a loss until Helen, with a few simple, calm, wise words arranges their lives and separates them for ever.

Or there is another feature: *My gal Sunday*. This gal Sunday is a Midwesterner, born on a Sunday and much later married to an English lord, a certain Lord Henry (Henry being his Christian name). The problem is: can the little Midwestern gal be happy with the rich English lord? They have lived together for twelve years, have innumerable children, I believe, but the problem is still unsolved. Lord Henry gets into trouble every week; all his friends are murdered, he is always suspected of killing them off but in the last moment his innocence is always proved and Lord Henry returns from jail to his beloved Sunday, spends a quiet weekend with her and next Monday commits a new murder. Few members of the British aristocracy spend so much time in jail as Lord Henry. Little wonder he can never spare a minute to drop into the House of Lords to take part in a Foreign Affairs debate.

(5) Quiz programmes are popular, too. A few members of the audience make fools of themselves in one way or another and in return they receive prizes.

And what prizes! Whenever you see a person carrying a refrigerator or a piano on his back or leading a camel through the streets of New York, you may rest assured that he has just won a quiz prize. Here is a notice I copied out from a New York paper:

Mrs William H. MacC. of Lock Haven, Pa, won $17,590 in prizes on Saturday night by correctly identifying Clara Bow, one time screen 'it' girl, as the mysterious 'Mrs Hush' on NBC's *Truth or Consequences* programme. The solver of the eight-week-old radio mystery won an airplane, an automobile, a week-end in New York, a week's vacation in Idaho, a year's maid service, a completely equipped trailer and a coat of paint, inside and out, for her house.

(6) There are some excellent and intelligent radio-commentators on the air. They are brave and candid and give balanced views on world events. One of these, in spite of the fact that his *Hooper Ratings* were the highest among all commentators and even higher than a great number of musical shows, was taken off the air by a commercial firm because of his mildly leftish tendencies. To use the immense cultural possibilities of radio mainly for the purpose of persuading people to buy more shirts, canned fruit, laxatives and boot polish is 'freedom of speech'; to take a brilliant commentator off the air because he says what he believes to be the truth is 'freedom of private enterprise'.

(7) But the main features are, of course, the commercials. They are declaimed in prose and recited in verse, sung by soloists and choirs, persuading, cajoling, threatening, warning and ordering people to buy X underwear or Y tinned beans. Every performance, except the sacred baseball match commentaries, is interrupted to tell you that you will become ravishingly beautiful if you eat Z cheese or else that you are sure to die young, poor and neglected if you do not use U shoe polish. One advertisement tells you in effect, that if you use a certain perfume, you become so irresistibly desirable that people will rape you in Fifth Avenue. You are told that honest men use only Akropolis fountain pens and a minute later that no decent person would touch anything but Muse fountain pens. One Texas radio station carried 2,215 commercials in 133 broadcasting hours, an average of 16·7 per hour. Once during a performance of *King Lear*, the tragedy flowed on in its majesty until at its climax King Lear broke loose in a ferocious malediction, condemning all his daughters for not drinking 'Optimus' orange juice for breakfast.

In short, the basic principles of broadcasting are these:

The main cultural aim is to sell more cheese to the public than it can consume.

Freedom of speech means freedom of great commercial firms to pull down all the rest of the people to their own intellectual level.

News is free; commercials are sacred.

'And get this: wear a "Trufit" truss, or else—!'

COMICS AND THE REST

I ALWAYS felt slightly insulted when I bought a newspaper in America. For three or four cents (there *The Times* is cheaper than any other paper) the newsvendor handed over a bulky volume of about eighty pages and I hadn't the slightest hope of reading more of it than the headlines and a few paragraphs here and there. What would you feel if on entering a restaurant and ordering roast beef, the waiters were to bring you three whole oxen with half a ton of Idaho potatoes (an Idaho potato is as large as a sizable marrow), or if you asked for a Frankfurter and six waiters dragged up a fourteen-yard long pole of meat and placed an ancient yataghan and a pitchfork beside your plate? I always felt just as you would feel in such a case whenever I received the usual overdose of my morning paper. I had to read it in a hurry, almost in a panic, because the evening papers are published early and if one loses any precious time, one can never catch up with it again. A friend of mine, a visitor from Tahiti, once remarked to me:

'In a month's time I'll go back to Tahiti. There, you know, we have a two-page news sheet published daily. It gives only the gist of world events and each item consists of two or three lines. No baseball, no sensational licence cases, no boxing matches, no murder stories and no twelve column reports on unimportant speeches by unimportant politicians. Just the gist of the news, fairly balanced and written in a rather dull manner, with the aloofness of a detached observer. I'll go back to Tahiti and there I shall know once again what is happening in New York.'

As far as I could make out, in America nobody reads political news in any case. Women read the advertisements only; schoolchildren the comic strips, also called—for some

unknown reason—the 'funnies'; well-dressed people read
the sports news and people in rags read only the stock exchange report. (Or, may be, *vice versa*: people who read
the stock exchange reports only, are always clad in rags.)

Apart from the size, American papers differ but little
from the newspapers of other lands. On the whole, perhaps, they are better informed and not quite as carefully
written as . . . well, offhand I can think of only ten newspapers in the whole world which are really carefully
written. American papers have correspondents in every
important city of the world and every correspondent is
anxious to make a scoop. Consequently they telegraph or
telephone home the 'real background' of and the 'inside
information' on all past and future political events—full
of the 'human touch'—and cases have definitely been
registered in the annals of journalism when these inside
stories were closely related to the truth.

I should like to enumerate a few points which struck me:

(1) There are no national dailies in the United
States. Distances are too vast for any paper to cover
the whole country. Magazines, on the other hand, can
cover the whole national market and their circulation
runs into astronomical figures. Well, magazines are
magazines. But there is a special kind of American
magazine—the *New Yorker* is the prototype—written by
grown ups for grown ups, with witty cartoons, amusing
stories and biting comments on current events. I
believe that England would do well with such a periodical. I do not wish to hurt the feelings of *Punch*
which *is* brilliantly written and always on a high level;
but I feel the time has come when somebody should

tell the editor that Lord Beaconsfield is no longer in office and tactfully inform him of the regrettable death of Queen Victoria.

(2) The digests are in a category of their own. The *Reader's Digest* is almost compulsory for everyone. Its sale exceeds thirteen million copies monthly, not counting the numerous foreign editions and the editions for the blind, the deaf and the illiterate. *Reader's Digest* is, after the Bible, the most widely circulated publication in the world.

People, after all, have little time to read and when they read these digests, they have the feeling of having read everything worth looking into. There is no subject the *Reader's Digest* will not touch, from baseball to religion, from cancer to dancing, from the art of happiness to the life of a salmon and from the higher education of the silk-worm to the hair-net industry in North China. All its articles are 'condensed' from some other newspaper or periodical, and the reader consequently gets everything in a dehydrated form— skinned, stoned and castrated. He only has to put these articles into a glass of water and when they are dissolved, drink them quickly and he gets a dose of culture. Many articles are ordered by the *Reader's Digest*, edited by its numerous editors (the periodical has about three editors for each article published) and printed in a satellite paper from which the *Digest* then reprints them in a condensed form. Occasionally these 'planted' articles are condensed in such a way that they are considerably longer than the article they are condensed from and it also happens occasionally that the 'reprint' appears a few days before the original.

'Dizzy's got the push!'

There are other popular digests in America—but of course, nothing to compare with the *Reader's Digest*. There are digests to deal with every subject under the sun—sport, agricultural, movie, international, Wild West, Negro and music digests—and it is little wonder that a business man I met was seriously considering publishing a *Digest of Digests* condensing all the condensed articles.

(3) In the last few years breasts have been discovered in America in general and in the American press in particular. I mean, the fact has been noticed by some journalists (nothing can remain hidden from these people) that women have breasts, usually two per woman. A young lady has become a Hollywood star mainly because she succeeded in securing more than her fair share in breasts. Many New York papers describe women in this way: 'The name of the young lady is Miss Eleanor W., aged 21, hair brown, height 5' 4", bust 34".' Reading these New York papers carefully you may improve your historical knowledge considerably and usefully as you learn the bust measurement of every woman from Sarah (Mrs Abraham) to Mme Tojo.

(4) The last phenomenon I wish to mention is the comic strips. They are called comic strips because they are neither comic nor strips. Just as a foreigner, coming to England, takes years to understand the British passion for queueing or tepid beer or the fact that a strongly Conservative newspaper can allow a left wing cartoonist to attack the paper's and its proprietor's policy in its own columns—so no visitor in the United States can understand the fascination and magic of these comic strips for so many millions. With the single exception of the *New York Times* no New York daily can forgo the comics, including the high ranking *New York Herald Tribune* and the ambitious *P.M.* The dailies run the comics in instalments, some giving two, three or four pages to them. On Sundays they are printed in colour and the coloured sheets are taken out of their usual place and put right on top of the front page, because, after all, it is the comics that sell the paper.

Once a stationer asked me in astonishment:

'What do you say? There are no comics in England?'

'That's what I said.'

'Good Heavens! How can they sell the papers then?'

I could not answer his query but after this conversation I spent a very uneasy night dreaming of *The Times*, the *Manchester Guardian* and the *Daily Telegraph* full of comic strips.

Some of the comics relate the adventures of various supermen who dress like athletes or circus acrobats. (This does not, apparently, cause the slightest surprise in Fifth Avenue.) They beat up everybody, knock out former boxing champions, solve all the riddles of the universe, defend the innocent and punish the guilty. Others tell the story of little girls or fairies, others of Texan cowboys, young suffering maidens, sportsmen, criminals, jockeys, master detectives and master killers. People keep talking in these strips, a flood of conversation bubbles out of their mouths and they put their deep problems in a very cute and brilliantly intelligent way, such as (I quote verbatim):

D

A man is unfair to himself, don't you agree, when he shows dumb loyalty to a girl he merely thinks he loves . . . when he knows that *another* girl, one who has *just come into his life* perhaps, is the girl he *really* loves? [Italics from the original.]

Whenever I discussed the problems of these strips, I was told by newspapermen and others that they have an immense educational value. If they alluded to the fact that they teach people good ju-jitsu tricks, marvellous ways to set houses on fire and how to steal

horses in Texas, I see their point. Otherwise I do not, but I take their word for it.

However much I write about comics, it will not convey a clear picture to the reader who is not familiar with the subject. I think an example is necessary, so the two authors of this book will try to give you one illustrating the nature and, at the same time, the immense educational value of the comics. Here we give you the chapter on Pythagoras from Mr Bertrand Russell's book *A History of Western Philosophy*:

III. BLACK AND WHITE

'FOR WHITES ONLY'

DEMOCRACY is a reality in America. It is, however, like a beautiful woman with a long, crooked nose or with a few teeth missing. It is democracy with a hitch. The Negroes are the black spot of America.

The world is a wicked place and the poor Americans are so busy defending the rights of Hindus in Pakistan, Moslems in India, Jews in Palestine, Koreans in Japan, Italians in Yugoslavia and Hungarians in Czechoslovakia that they simply cannot give a thought to Negroes in the United States.

There are well over twelve million Negroes in the U.S. —that is, more than the whole population of Canada. Almost ten million of them live in the so-called Southern States, which are, roughly speaking, the South-Eastern States. On the other hand, there are seven states where the number of Negroes is under one thousand. Now, obviously, the Southerners are the great experts on the Negro problem and they will explain to you that the crimes of Negroes are terrible and manifold and their persecution justified.

(1) First of all, the Negro is black. This seems to be one of his main crimes and is held very much against him. A great number of Southerners would be much more tolerant with the Negro, if only he were not black. When discussing the Negro question with white

Southerners, I heard the horrified remark innumerable times:

'But don't you see, they are black!'

I must admit there is a great deal of truth in this very able observation: the Negroes *are* black—no use denying it.

(2) They are illiterate or at least uneducated. I believe this second charge is slightly old-fashioned and should be replaced by a new one. It is a very old recipe to exclude people from schools or keep them in the utmost poverty so that they should be unable to go to school and then accuse them of being uneducated.

(3) They are over-ambitious and pushing—they learn too much.

(4) They are full of racial prejudice. Millions of them are satisfied with their situation, they believe in their own inferiority and have a strong dislike of Negroes coming from the North and talking about a real abolition of slavery. I should go so far as to state that some of them even like being lynched. Not all of them and not all the time—just a few Negroes, every now and then, let us say twice a year, in the height of the season.

(5) They do not 'keep in their place'. So-called fair-minded Southerners told me that they have nothing against those Negroes who know their place, they only object to the 'uppity' ones. In other words they are perfectly adorable as long as they remain servants, janitors, waiters, sewage cleaners, boot-blacks, unskilled manual workers (preferably receiving very low wages). The trouble starts only when they talk of freedom and equality and other outrageous things of

The position of the Negro in American society

this nature and do not honour their white masters (in many cases illiterate, bad-mannered, white coolies).

(6) They stink. Negroes—mostly those who do not wash for several weeks on end—have a peculiar smell of their own. I met a great number of white Southerners who were too busy to spend much time in washing and I dare say I could tell them without difficulty from a rose in full bloom.

(7) Their fathers were slaves. Note: this is the shame of the Negroes and not of their masters.

(8) They have criminal tendencies. There are indeed some ugly crimes—lynching for instance—in which Negroes are involved without fail, in one way or another.

These are the crimes the Negroes are charged with. Yes, their persecution *would* be justified but, of course, there is no persecution at all. The Fifteenth Amendment of the Constitution declares:

> The right of the citizens of the United States to vote shall not be denied or abridged by the United States or by any State on account of race, color, or previous condition of servitude.

This rule is scrupulously adhered to and Negroes are not deprived of their franchise on account of their race and colour but they are deprived of it by the use of various devices such as the poll tax and white primary laws.

Then there is segregation in the South but the principle is: separate but equal. In buses for instance the front places are reserved for white men, that is true, but on the other hand, the back places are reserved for Negroes. (Should you sit among Negroes, the driver will refuse to start.) On every train there are Jim Crow cars—cars reserved for Negroes—usually just behind the engine so that they should get a fair amount of smoke, while the rest of the train is reserved for white passengers. If Negroes are crowded together in a dangerous and unhealthy way while each white passenger has seven seats for himself, that is just bad luck, but they will not change the arrangements. It is true that Negroes are excluded from restaurants, hotels, cinemas, theatres, hospitals and many other public places, but, in turn, white men do not frequent Negro establishments. Negroes are excluded from many shops and even when the white owner graciously condescends to accept their money, he forbids them to try on hats, suits and gloves in many States. Negroes cannot get into a restaurant car, or book a place in a sleeper or in a pullman car but they are fully entitled to stay out. It is easy to see that these arrangements are just and fair, worthy of the defendants of all minorities, provided the minorities are far away, in other people's countries. Separate and equal: all Negroes are quite separate and all Negroes are equal.

The real issue is, as many people explained it to me, the freedom of the whites. They must be free to have parks, hospitals, libraries for whites only, provided that other equally good parks etc are reserved for negroes, too. If you ask Southerners whether Negroes do have equally good parks, libraries and hospitals, they will laugh their heads off as this is considered a capital joke. White people must be free to keep Negroes out of their own restaurants by various devices and now, at last, they have received the legal right of lynching, too. Until now, there was some doubt in many

'It is your duty, gentlemen, to reach a verdict simply and solely according to the evidence that is put before you, to banish from your minds all consideration of extraneous circumstances, to preserve complete and absolute impartiality, to uphold without fear or favor the integrity of the Law and the sacred right of every citizen of the United States—the right to a FAIR TRIAL. While there is nothing in our Constitution against the acquittal of a negro . . .'

white minds as to whether lynching was really lawful. In May 1947 twenty eight white men were indicted and tried (for the first time in the history of the South) for lynching a Negro youth. Sixteen persons out of twenty eight had admitted in signed statements that they had taken part in the lynching, but an all-white jury acquitted all the defendants on every one of the ninety eight charges. They returned their verdict in five and a half hours—giving about three and a half minutes to each count. The jury, of course, was supposed to decide a question of fact only, but the South interpreted this verdict as a general permit for lynching and a few hours later another Negro was duly lynched by a white mob.

The North is a Paradise, compared with the South. There are no Jim Crow cars there, Negroes have the right to vote and often are employed together with white people, doing the same jobs. But they are unable to get an apartment anywhere except in Harlem (though a negligible number live in Brooklyn, in the Bronx and Greenwich Village). They have to pay exorbitant prices in overcrowded slums, they cannot hire rooms in hotels and they are excluded from most of the restaurants and many other public places— although, every now and then, the managers of hotels and restaurants are fined for excluding them. Whenever I went out to have lunch or dinner with a Negro, I had to ask him to choose a place and even so, many inquisitive or hostile looks were thrown at us. Even the workers follow suit. While C.I.O. specifically forbids discrimination, there are a great number of American Federation of Labour Unions which exclude Negroes by provision of their Constitution, others which exclude them by tacit consent and others again which afford them only segregated auxiliary status.

The law may say whatever it likes; a few high-minded judges may pronounce judgments inspired by the noblest sentiments; a gradually enlightened and increasingly worried public opinion may try to exercise pressure, but the wall of prejudice seems to be impenetrable. The owner of a restaurant will say to a Negro that all his tables are booked; or if a Negro succeeds in finding a place he will instruct his waiters not to serve him. Then the owner withdraws into a corner and continues a heated argument with his friends about the problem of the Macedonian minority not enjoying equal rights in Bulgaria or the Jews not being fairly treated in Palestine. Should he allow Negroes to eat at his place, he would lose many white clients; should the owner of a house let apartments to Negroes, the price of his estate— and all estates in the neighbourhood—would fall. Should such a danger arise, all estate agents would appeal to the racial pride of the public, organise demonstrations and shout high-minded slogans to save the estate prices. It is true that this treatment of the Negro is against the spirit and the letter of the Constitution and it is true that the Constitution is sacred. But the Dollar is more sacred. High should be our reverence for the Constitution; but estate prices should be higher.

During the war, Negroes were allowed to serve in the United States armed forces but segregation was fully enforced. The Negroes served in separate units and lived in separate barracks. Apart from minor details, the only major exception from the segregation rules was that German and Japanese bullets were not marked: 'For Whites Only.'

Prejudices cut too deep—many people say—and there is no solution. I believe there *is* a solution. As soon as the presence of Negroes increases estate prices instead of lowering them, all the walls of segregation will fall down.

THE SAME IN BLACK

IF you walk around in Harlem—in the black Metropolis, or leaving euphemism apart for a moment, in the black ghetto of New York—you can see an interesting and much-discussed racial problem reflected in the windows of beauty parlours and women's shops. You will see all kinds of dummies, just as in the windows of similar establishments all the world over. But *these* dummies are black. Black-faced dummies with wiry and sometimes curly hair proclaim the skill of the hairdresser or dressmaker. Then you notice a great number of shops with white dummies only; then some with creole dummies; and then again other windows where black dummies are carefully mixed with white ones.

Negroes cannot quite decide whether they should be dark or light. Race conscious people are proud of being dark and look down upon the lighter ones, who obviously have some white blood—and this is, in fact, the truth in the case of two thirds of Harlem's inhabitants. Others, on the other hand, look down upon the dark ones and would do anything in their power to lighten their skins. Negro newspapers preach racial consciousness but at the same time are compelled to advertise ointments which are supposed to make one's skin lighter.

Harlem is the black variation of New York. The Negroes are Americans first and Negroes only in the second place.

Snobbery is a complicated enough business, as it is, for white Americans. But it is child's play compared with the task facing a dark-skinned snob.

If you are a Negro and wish to be a snob, you have to distinguish between extra-racial and intra-racial snobbery. Extra-racial snobbery is, of course, a natural and probably quite justified reaction to being persecuted and oppressed. If you want to be a proper Negro in New York, you must

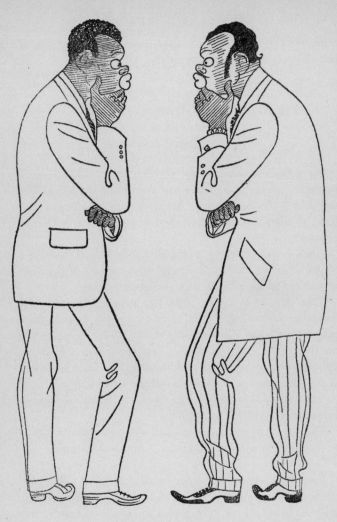

To be or not to be . . .

study the following rules as they contain the minimum of knowledge you can get along with.

Extra-racial snobbery

You may (*a*) hate all white people,
     (*b*) ignore them, or
     (*c*) adore and envy them.

But whatever you choose, imitate them. Imitate their manners, smoke their long cigars, wear their red-and-green-and-golden ties and even understand their anti-Negro attitude, at least, against certain classes or groups of the Negro population.

Once I was taken by a white lady friend of mine to a Negro club for backward youths where a boy of fourteen acquainted us with his racial theories and plans:

'One day we are going into the streets,' he said in a dreaming voice—'We shall carry long, long knives, dripping with blood. We are going to kill all the white people on that night. All of them. You too, Miss Catherine, although you are very nice and sweet to us.' Then he looked at me and added politely: 'And all the visitors, too.'

'How can you say things like that?' my friend exclaimed, surprised and a little terrified.

The boy looked at us and replied with an angelic smile:

'I am so young, Miss Catherine. And so backward.'

You must oppose all inter-racial marriages. You will come across very few of those, at any rate. Sometimes you will find brave people, Negro men and white women or vice versa, who fall in love with each other and are prepared to defy all racial barriers. Fairly often, you will see a poor white girl who sells herself to a rich Negro. The marriage of a white man to a Negro girl is a much rarer occurrence. Whatever the reason for the marriage, the white partner becomes a Negro in the eyes of the white community and all his or her children are considered Negroes. He remains however the white stranger and intruder in the eyes of the Negroes. They take up a 'we are not honoured' attitude. I personally consider this attitude ignoble, mean and revengeful, but, good Heavens, would I share it if I were a Negro!

Apart from having a general attitude to whites, you may despise certain groups. The nineteenth century British antagonism to the Irish, for instance, still survives in Black New England and beyond its boundaries. Nowadays, however, it is much more fashionable to be an anti-Semite. Harlem's white shop keepers and landlords are said to be mostly Jews and they are not hated as white men or as shop-keepers and landlords, but as Jews.

The story goes around in New York that a very black Negro woman tried on a hat with a lot of fruit and flowers and other decorations on it, looked at herself in the mirror and, horrified, exclaimed:

'My goodness, don't I look Jewish!'

Intra-racial snobbery

The doctrine of intra-racial snobbery is much more difficult to absorb.

First of all there is the difference in money, culture and profession. The dividing line between rich and poor seems to be much stronger than all racial bonds.

The Negroes of lighter shade look down upon very dark Negroes.

Very dark Negroes look down upon lighter ones—in this connection you must remember that there is no shade between pitch-black and light creole, mixed with yellow, red and even green that is not represented in Harlem. Real, full-blooded African Negroes who migrated recently into the United States from Nigeria, the Gold Coast, Congo, Liberia and similar countries or colonies, look down upon all American Negroes, because they consider themselves the aristocracy of the race and, in fact, you can find some Negro princes in their ranks.

Then there are all the Negro emigrants and refugees. After all, America is such a rich and generous mother that even her step-sons can live a better and fuller life than many of them could in their country of origin. One quarter of Harlem's population forms Black New England. The Black New Englanders are proud Britishers who resent racial discrimination, which they hardly knew (except the Jamaicans), keep their British nationality, celebrate whenever some joyful event occurs in the British royal family, speak a kind of Americanised and colonised cockney, play a large and important part in Harlem's cultural life, smile at everybody and are jeered at by everybody else.

There are the Haitians who come from an independent Negro republic, where white men are a tolerated minority but treated in a much nobler fashion than Negroes are usually treated by white men.

There are the Spanish-speaking coloured men, chiefly the Puerto Ricans, who suffer discrimination from the whites and try to keep the balance by discriminating against the Negroes.

There are the French-speaking Negroes, who arrived from various French possessions, mix much more freely

The position of the American in Haitian society

with white Frenchmen than any other group in the community mixes with any white group and celebrate the anniversary of the fall of the Bastille every year.

Then there are the Moslem Negroes and the half-caste Negro-Indians, Negro-Chinese, Negro-Filipino and Negro-Malayan mixtures and finally, among other millions of native American Negroes, the ancient tribe of Negro Jews, about ten thousand of them, who have practised Judaism for thousands of years, read the *Talmud Torah*, send their children to *Yeshivos*, eat *kosher* dishes only, do not work on Saturdays, faithfully follow their bearded rabbi and are very clever in business. A number of them speak Yiddish only. Some people believe that it is a slight exaggeration to be a Negro and a Jew rolled into one and suggest that they should choose: either-or. The Negro Jews are not the Jews of the Negro community, in the European sense of the word, but they are clannish themselves, and do not call themselves Negroes, but Ethiopians or Afro-Americans or Isro-Africans.

This classification is, of course, over-simplified. There are very many Negroes who bear their hard lot with much courage and intelligence. Basically, however, there is a great deal of truth in my classification. I believe, that if the Negroes were not snobs, discrimination against them would be justified; things as they are only prove that the Negroes are not better or worse than the rest of the community or than the rest of us.

IV. MILD AND BITTER

THE STATES OF THE UNION

NINE years ago, soon after my arrival in England, a friend of mine invited me to an international football match. 'International?' I asked him. 'Against whom? France?' 'Oh no,' he replied, 'that wouldn't be interesting. Wales.' I was very much surprised to hear that an English-Welsh match was called an 'international'. My English friends, to whom I told this 'story', did not quite see what I was talking about. By now, of course, I know very well what all Continentals are apt to forget, that Great Britain is inhabited by three nations.

Most British, in the same way, are inclined to forget that the United States is not one huge country, but in fact, a federation of forty eight states. In addition to the forty eight states there is District of Columbia, better known as Washington D.C.

Some of the states detest one another wholeheartedly. A New Jersey man once explained to me what a pity it was they could not ally themselves with Connecticut and invade New York.

'What a shame,' I said sympathetically, 'that you haven't an army.'

'Why,' he replied, 'of course our state has its own militia.'

In some states you will find an over-developed local patriotism. The inhabitants of Texas are very nationalistic indeed. A number of Texas soldiers took part, for instance, in the invasion of France in 1944, whereupon one of the Texan papers came out with the headlines: 'TEXANS

INVADE NORMANDY'. There is a great antipathy between South and North and some Southerners still believe that the North treats them as a defeated nation and exploits them as a market; on the other hand Northerners—the Yankees—believe that the South should treat the Negroes better. People, who to my ear had exactly the same accent, jeer at one another because of their pronunciation.

In a recent book, edited by Dick Hyman and entitled *Looney Laws*, certain regulations, still in force in various states are collected and I should like to mention a few examples.

Some laws to maintain public decency

In Minnesota men's and women's underwear must not hang on the same clothes line.

In Elkhart, Indiana, there is a law against barbers threatening to cut off children's ears.

In St Joseph, Missouri, city firemen must not walk about in their underwear.

In Gary, Indiana, it is against the law to ride in a tramway within four hours of eating garlic.

In Monrie, Utah, it is illegal to dance with a girl unless daylight can be seen between you.

In Indiana it is forbidden to seduce a young lady while teaching her to roller skate.

For the defence of animals

In Maine it is against the law to set fire to a mule.

In Baltimore, Maryland, it is a penal offence to torture an oyster.

In Kentucky the shooting of clay pigeons during the breeding season is prohibited.

Strictly legal

In Alabama, if you have not been a resident for a year, you can be jailed for having salt water shrimps in your possession.

In California it is a penal offence to set a trap for mice unless you have a hunting licence.

In Seattle, Washington, goldfish must not ride in city buses unless they lie still.

In Louisville, Kentucky, it is prohibited to shoot fish with a bow and arrow.

In Joliet, Illinois, a woman can be jailed for trying on more than six garments in one shop.

Miscellaneous

In Sault Ste Marie, Michigan, it is a misdemeanour to spit against the wind.

In Kentucky no woman may appear in a bathing suit unless armed with a club.

In Arkansas, it is illegal to mispronounce the name of Arkansas. (By the way, for your convenience, it is pronounced: Ahr-kan-saw.)

In Mohave, Arizona, anyone caught stealing soap, must wash himself with it until all the soap is used up.

In Jonesboro, Georgia, it is against the law to say: 'Oh Boy!'

Public safety

In Fort Madison, Iowa, the fire department must practise for fifteen minutes before going to extinguish a fire.

Traffic law

In New Hampshire 'when two motor vehicles meet at an intersection, each shall come to a full stop and neither shall proceed until the other has gone.'

It would be easy to elaborate on this subject and make fun of the diversity of laws, regulations and customs in the various American states. The fact, however, that these American states succeeded in abolishing all possibility of going to war with one another and in establishing a great union is a tremendous achievement and an example for the whole world, especially for the United Nations. It was not such a very long time ago that people were declaring that to imagine that the various North American States could live under the same government was a naïve and utopian dream; just as people say today that it is a naïve and utopian dream that Soviet Russia and Peru, for instance, should obey the same central authority. The very existence of the United States, like that of the British Commonwealth of Nations, is a proof of great wisdom, toleration and statesmanship. My above-quoted New Jersey friend, however, once remarked:

'It is easy for the British to live together in peace. Australia is thousands of miles away from England. But New York is just across the river.'

THE RULERS

IN England you know for instance that the Labour Party is for the nationalisation of various industries and the Conservatives are against it. In America such ideological clashes hardly ever occur. A practical issue may be whether the U.S. should give a large loan to Britain or not. In Siloam Springs (Ala) the loyal Democratic leader, with an eye on the Jewish inhabitants, may take up an anti-British attitude because of Palestine. In the next village, however, the bank manager's daughter may have an English fiancé, a former R.A.F. pilot, who is personally very popular and the Democratic Party leader will be inclined to say: 'Let the poor boy have the dough'.

All this may seem very confusing but, in fact, it is quite simple. The difference between the two main American parties is very sharp and well defined; it is more marked than the difference between Communists and right wing Democrats in any European coalition government:

(a) one party is in, the other is out;
(b) one party wants to stay in and the other tries to get it out.

(After all, in nine cases out of ten, what is the real source of a minister's greatness? Not his political convictions, not his ideas, not his speeches, not his reforms and not his bills, but the simple fact that he *is* a minister. And the greatest contrast to being a minister is not being a minister.)

Beyond and above all political parties stand two layers of society who really rule the United States of America. First of all the women. There are no American 'Dubarrys'. It is not the old *cherchez la femme* story. It is *cherchez l'argent*. Women as a rule do not work and they are supposed to spend nine-tenths of all the money spent in the whole

The Tories are against it

country. This fact places immense social, economic and political power in their hands. American society is a matriarchal society. Useless males are not exterminated as they used to be by certain tribes in Formosa; they are only condemned to manufacture useless things (such as certain types of novels and magazines, nearly all the films, cosmetics, radio programmes etc). Men are condemned to wear golden ties and socks with silver circles on them. If the poor males succeed in making some money, women systematically establish charity clubs to spend it in the most ingenious ways. The majority of these clubs propagate the noblest ideas and support very good causes; some others are latecomers on the field of charity. It is due to the women that many an American university or college is transformed (as Charles and Mary Beard put. it) into ' a small school attached to a vast stadium'.

There is one class which stands even higher than women: children. All things are permitted to children. They may beat one another black and blue in the park and nobody dares to interfere. You may see one little boy kneeling on another, hitting his head on the asphalt pavement as hard as he can and repeating. 'D'you give in?' He will go on doing it until the other yells: 'I give in,' then he gets up, and the affair is duly settled. You must not interfere because children are sacred. The second little boy, lying on the pavement, is sacred, too; still, you must not interfere. I saw a little girl of fourteen reading poetry to a traffic policeman on the corner of Broadway and 44th Street. The policeman was desperate but he had to listen attentively. At Christmas time a million dollars worth of toys are destroyed in the department stores by children who try them out, but this is included in the expenses. When the *Missouri* (the battleship on which the Japanese armistice treaty was signed) was shown to the public and visitors were allowed on board, American children did more damage to her in one day than the combined Japanese navy and air force had ever hoped to do.

THE Americans are decent and good-hearted people. In Hungary we used to define a truly generous person as one who would give you his last shirt if you needed it. This definition would not fit the American. But if you have no shirt he would lend you some money to buy one, provided

  (a) you buy it from him and
  (b) you are not a Communist.

(In many cases a Communist is defined as a man who has no shirt.)

Prosperity makes America the country of unlimited possibilities. As too many people want to read there and many people can afford to spend a quarter on printed matter of one sort or another, more illiterate people live on their pen in America than the total number of illiterates in other, less fortunate countries.

The Americans have their own arts. Jazz is their music, comic strips their most admired pictures, magazine stories their literature, Hollywood films their most popular entertainment, skyscrapers their architecture and their newest ball-point pens can write under water. America is immensely rich, her people are steadily growing in number and they are—as prosperous people always are—kind, good, fair, generous and keen-minded. They feel that they have inherited a world and they are eager to lead it to new destinies.

They trust themselves because they are confident that they can mass-produce many more orange squeezers, electric potato peelers and yellow socks with green circles on them, for the benefit of all humanity. We know, too,

The position of the American in his own estimation. The curvature of the earth's surfaces renders it impossible to observe this position without some distortion of perspective. The possible margin of error in the above diagram is about the width of the Atlantic Ocean

that God could make America a wonderful country if he only had the money.

*   *   *

But can we trust them as leaders? . . . When I was a small boy we used to play football every Saturday afternoon in the field (it would be called the village green in England). Our centre forward was always the same little boy, let's call him Sammy. There was always a great deal of argument as to who should be in the team and what position one or another boy should occupy. But there was never any argument about the position of the centre-forward. It had to be Sammy. He was not a very good player; he could not use his left foot at all. But he wanted to play centre-forward and centre-forward he played.

The ball belonged to him.